The Ultimate Quiz Book

Sport

The Ultimate Quiz Book

Sport

Andrew Langley

**MARKS &
SPENCER**

Marks and Spencer p.l.c.
PO Box 3339
Chester CH99 9QS

shop online
www.marksandspencer.com

Produced by Design Principals
Front Cover image: Photo by Dennis Oulds/Central Press/ © Getty Images)

ISBN 978-1-84805-913-9
Printed in China

CONTENTS

FOOTBALL: HOME
QUESTIONS 1–24

TENNIS
QUESTIONS 25–44

RACING & SPEED
QUESTIONS 45–64

RUGBY
QUESTIONS 65–84

ATHLETICS
QUESTIONS 85–104

CRICKET
QUESTIONS 105–124

GOLF
QUESTIONS 125–144

FOOTBALL: AWAY
QUESTIONS 145–160

OTHER TEAM SPORTS
QUESTIONS 161–180

OTHER INDIVIDUAL SPORTS
QUESTIONS 181–200

FOOTBALL: HOME
ENGLAND

1

How many clean sheets did Gordon Banks keep in 73 internationals?

2

How many goals did Brian and Nigel Clough score for England?

3

Who was the first Channel Islander to play for England?

4

Who did England beat 7-0 at Wembley in 1973?

5

How many hat-tricks did Jimmy Greaves score for England?

6

Against whom did Robbie Fowler score his first England goal?

7

In which year did England play their first ever international?

8

Which team did England beat 4-0 in March 2009?

9

Who was England's "Player of the Tournament" at the 2006 World Cup?

10

In which year did Alan Shearer retire from international football?

11

Who won the Germany v England "Battle of Berlin" in 1938?

12

In which year did Bobby Charlton make his England debut?

FOOTBALL: HOME
TECHNICAL TERMS

1

What is the "back pass rule"?

2

What is the Italian term for a sweeper?

3

What is a "silver goal"?

4

What's the term for putting the ball between an opponent's legs?

5

What is the "onion bag"?

6

Which game derives its name from the Spanish for "indoor football"?

7

Which ruling in 1995 removed the limit on foreign players in EU clubs?

8

What is the name of Germany's top professional league?

9

What is the term for the markings at the pitch corners?

10

What name does the word "soccer" come from?

11

What is the "back door" of a goal?

12

What is another name for the 3 – 5 – 1 formation?

FOOTBALL: HOME
NAME THE YEAR (1)

1

When did Chelsea win their second European Cup-winners' Cup Final?

2

When did Rangers complete their first "treble"?

3

In which year did Italy gain their first win at Wembley?

4

When was the first Wembley stadium opened to the public?

5

When did Luton switch their pitch to plastic?

6

In which year did Leeds United win their first league championship?

7

When did Bobby Moore become the youngest captain to lift the FA Cup?

8

When was the League Cup first held at the new Wembley Stadium?

9

When did Frank Stapleton make the first of five Cup Final appearances?

10

When did Peter Shilton play his first League match?

11

When did Liverpool complete a hat-trick of League Championships?

12

In which year did Bury win the FA Cup without conceding a goal?

FOOTBALL: HOME
FA CUP (1)

1

Who recorded the biggest win in an FA Cup Final?

2

Who was just 21 when he captained Leicester's 1969 Cup Final team?

3

Which two Second Division clubs reached the Final in the 1980s?

4

Who scored Chelsea's winning goal in the 2000 Final?

5

Which Scottish international kept goal for Tottenham in 1961 and 1962?

6

Who came from 0-3 to win 4-3 against Southampton in 2001?

7

Which team has won the FA Cup most times?

8

Which player heads the FA Cup goal-scoring table?

9

What FA Cup record was set by Bournemouth's Ted MacDougall in 1971?

10

Why do Portsmouth hold the record for longest period as Cup holders?

11

Who scored the fastest goal in a Cup Final?

12

How many times have Manchester United been beaten Cup Finalists?

FOOTBALL: HOME
RECORD BREAKERS

1

Who is the all-time leading scorer in the English Premiership?

2

Who has made the most Premiership appearances?

3

Who has made most international appearances for Scotland?

4

Which team has the most appearances in the FA Cup?

5

What English scoring record is held by Arthur Rowley?

6

Who scored most goals in an English league season?

7

Which Premiership team scored fewest home goals in a season?

8

Which team had the longest unbeaten run in a Premiership season?

9

Who appeared in most English league games?

10

Which Premiership team made the most points in a season?

11

Who scored most international goals for Wales?

12

Who has the most Premier League Winners Medals?

FOOTBALL: HOME
GOALSCORERS & GOALKEEPERS

1

How quick was the quickest goal in an English League game?

2

Who scored all four goals in a 2-2 draw in 1976?

3

With which club did Gordon Banks start his League playing career?

4

How old was Jimmy Greaves when he scored his 200th League goal?

5

Which Leeds goalkeeper once famously threw the ball into his own net?

6

Against which club did George Best score six times in 1970?

7

What was Bob Wilson's profession before he became a goalkeeper?

8

Which keeper has gone most Premiership games without conceding a goal?

9

In which seasons did Manchester United score most League goals?

10

Who scored the longest range goal in open play in the Premiership?

11

Which goalkeeper scored the longest range goal from a freekick?

12

How long has Bobby Charlton's record England goal tally stood?

FOOTBALL: HOME
NAME THE YEAR (2)

1

When did Maradona's "hand of God" knock England out of the World Cup?

2

In which year was the Football League increased to 92 clubs?

3

When was Robbie Fowler fined for mooning at Leicester City fans?

4

When was Tom Finney knighted?

5

In which year did Ryan Giggs makes his Manchester United debut?

6

Billy Bremner played his last game for Leeds in which year?

7

When did Bob Paisley win his first major trophy with Liverpool?

8

Which year's World Cup saw David Beckham sent off?

9

When did Portsmouth win the FA Cup?

10

In which year did Scotland's "Wembley Wizards" beat England 5-1?

11

When did Wigan Athletic reach the League's top tier for the first time?

12

When did Paul Gascoigne join Rangers?

1

[Of Jimmy Hill] "If there's a prat in the world, he's the prat."

2

[In 1970] "We have nothing to learn from Brazil."

3

"If Everton were playing in my garden, I'd draw the curtains."

4

"Football is a simple game and should be kept simple."

5

[Of Alf Ramsey] "A stubborn bugger."

6

[Of Jock Stein] "An iron fist without a velvet glove."

7

"If I walked on water, my accusers would say it's because I can't swim."

8

[Of Kenny Dalglish] "The moaningest Minnie I've ever known."

9

"If Kevin Keegan fell into the Tyne, he'd come up with a salmon in his mouth."

10

[Of Wimbledon] "The only hooligans here are the players."

11

[Of Nobby Stiles] "He's never hurt anyone. Mind you, he's frightened a few."

12

[Of Pat Crerand] "He's deceptive. He's slower than you think."

FOOTBALL: HOME
THE FOOTBALL LEAGUE

1

Which team gained only 8 points from 34 matches in 1904-07?

2

Which Liverpool fullback won eight League Championship medals?

3

Who won Championships with three teams in four successive years?

4

Who replaced Doncaster Rovers in the Football League in 1998?

5

Who went 30 games without a win in Division 3 in 1956-57?

6

For which team did Ernie Moss make over half his 749 appearances?

7

Which club went from Fourth Division to First and back between
1964 and 1987?

8

Who were relegated in 1938 despite scoring most First Division goals?

9

In which year did Accrington Stanley resign from the League?

10

Which two clubs have been Champions of all the old four Divisions?

11

With which two clubs did John McGovern win Championships in the 1970s?

12

Who were promoted from the Third Division in their first League season
in 1994?

FOOTBALL: HOME
REFEREES

. . . .

1

Who was David Beckham sent off for kicking in the 1998 World Cup?

. . . .

2

Which Newcastle player was fined for assaulting David Elleray in 1998?

. . . .

3

Who was Britain's first senior woman referee?

. . . .

4

How far, on average, does a referee run in a match?

. . . .

5

What was Mr A. Stair's claim to fame?

. . . .

6

In which year did an English referee first use a whistle?

. . . .

7

Which English referee dished out 8 red cards and 123 yellows in 2008/9?

. . . .

8

What happened to ref Melvin Sylvester when he punched a player in 2005?

. . . .

9

Who was England's only referee at the 1998 World Cup finals?

. . . .

10

What big mistake did ref Arthur Ellis make during a Rangers cup
tie in 1956?

. . . .

11

Who was the first referee to send a player off in an FA Cup Final?

. . . .

12

What big mistake did Ray Tinkler make in a 1971 Championship decider?

. . . .

FOOTBALL: HOME
NAME THE YEAR (3)

1

In which year was Glen Hoddle sacked as England manager?

2

In which year did Arsenal provide seven members of the England team?

3

In which year did Peter Shilton win his record 109th England cap?

4

When did Britain last win Olympic soccer gold?

5

When did Terry Paine make the last of 824 League appearances?

6

Which year was the "White Horse" Cup Final?

7

When was an Englishman first named European Player of the Year?

8

When did Liverpool win their first League title under Bob Paisley?

9

When did Jürgen Klinsmann join Spurs?

10

When was Bobby Charlton voted European Footballer of the Year?

11

When did Hungary crush England 6-3 at Wembley?

12

When did Billy Wright gain his 100th England cap?

FOOTBALL: HOME
THE PREMIERSHIP

. . . .

1

In which year was the Premier League founded?

. . . .

2

Which team has won most titles?

. . . .

3

Which team had fewest wins in a Premiership season?

. . . .

4

Who has made the most Premiership appearances for one club?

. . . .

5

Which two players share the goal-scoring record for a whole season?

. . . .

6

What record is shared by Patrick Vieira, Duncan Ferguson and Richard Dunne?

. . . .

7

How many touches did Keith Gillespie get before being sent off in 2007?

. . . .

8

Who left his partnership with Gerard Houllier in 1998?

. . . .

9

Who was Liverpool's top Premiership scorer in 2000/1?

. . . .

10

Which is the only team to concede 100 goals in a season?

. . . .

11

Who was George Graham's first signing for Tottenham?

. . . .

12

Who resigned as Manchester City chairman in 1993?

. . . .

FOOTBALL: HOME
SEEING RED

1

Which future England manager was sent off in an Under-23 match in 1972?

2

What is the record number of dismissals in one match?

3

Who was sent off against England in the 1966 World Cup quarter-finals?

4

Of which country was he captain?

5

Which Hearts players were sent off for fighting with each other in 1994?

6

Who was the first Welsh international to be sent off?

7

Which Arsenal player was banned for pushing a referee in 1997?

8

Which Bury player scored a hat-trick in 1973 and was then sent off?

9

Which Northern Ireland player was sent off at the 1982 World Cup finals?

10

Which two Leeds players were sent off at Highbury in 2001?

11

Who was sent off against Arsenal in a Champions' League semi-final?

12

Which Scottish striker was sent off against Wales in 1981?

FOOTBALL: HOME
FA CUP (2)

1

Who is the youngest player to score in an FA Cup Final?

2

Who made the most Cup Final appearances?

3

How many clubs competed for the Cup in the 2007/8 season?

4

Which tie attracted the highest Cup attendance of all time?

5

In which year did Dulwich Hamlet score 7 goals in a tie, yet lose?

6

Which team have appeared in a Final four times, yet never won?

7

Which 3rd Division side knocked Arsenal out of the Cup in 1965?

8

What was special about the 1986/7 quarter-finals?

9

Who is the only player to captain Scottish and English Cup winners?

10

Which 20th-century player gained four Cup-winner's medals?

11

Which manager took Everton to the 1995 Final?

12

Who was Man of the Match in the 2009 Cup Final?

FOOTBALL: HOME
MANCHESTER AND MERSEYSIDE

1

How many League goals did Denis Law score for United?

2

Which goalkeeper ended his career at Old Trafford with the treble in 1999?

3

Which United manager signed Ray Wilkins?

4

How many England caps did Colin Bell win?

5

When did Joe Mercer become City manager?

6

Who has made most League appearances for Manchester City?

7

How many times have Liverpool been relegated?

8

How many League goals did Ian Rush score for Liverpool?

9

Who played 843 games for Liverpool after a 1960 debut?

10

Which striker joined Everton from Rangers for £4 million in 1994?

11

Which former *Coronation Street* actor bought Everton?

12

Who beat Everton in the 1977 League Cup Final?

FOOTBALL: HOME
LONDON CLUBS

1

Who became Millwall manager in 1974?

2

Who is the youngest Millwall player to score a League hat-trick?

3

From which club did Fulham sign Allan Clarke?

4

In which year did Ian Wright make his Arsenal debut?

5

Who kept goal for Arsenal in the 1930 Cup Final?

6

Who scored Arsenal's goal in the 2001 Cup Final?

7

Who was Chelsea manager from 1988 to 1991?

8

Who made his Chelsea debut aged 16 in 1967?

9

How many England managers have played for Chelsea?

10

In which year did Spurs do the "double"?

11

Which of Spurs' Scottish internationals was killed by lightning in 1964?

12

Which player returned to Spurs as manager in 2001?

FOOTBALL: HOME
ODDITIES (1)

. . . .

1

Which League club does Tim Henman support?

. . . .

2

Which future Manchester United star was a French Cup winner in 1990?

. . . .

3

What was thrown at Graham Taylor by a Bolton fan in 1995?

. . . .

4

Which club has a fanzine called *The Oatcake*?

. . . .

5

Which player advertised Brut with Henry Cooper in the 1970s?

. . . .

6

Which Scottish club had a fanzine called *Mr Bismarck's Electric Pickelhaube*?

. . . .

7

Which country scored after 8 seconds against England in 1994?

. . . .

8

Which Midlands team were originally formed to play rugby?

. . . .

9

Who was the first foreigner to be voted England's Footballer of the Year?

. . . .

10

Which weirdly named team won the League of Wales in 2000?

. . . .

11

In which year did Scottish fans tear down the Wembley goalposts?

. . . .

12

How high is the new Wembley Arch?

. . . .

FOOTBALL: HOME
SCOTLAND

1

Who were the only country to defeat Scotland in the 1978 World Cup qualifiers?

2

How many Scotland caps did Alan Hansen win?

3

Who did Scotland beat 5-2 in their opening match at the 1982 World Cup?

4

Which club did Denis Law play for when he won his first Scotland cap?

5

Which Scottish international played for a German club in 1997?

6

Who scored Scotland's winner against Germany in April 1999?

7

Why doesn't the Scottish team play in the Olympics?

8

In which town did the first Scotland v England match take place?

9

What was the year?

10

When did Scotland play in their first World Cup?

11

Who managed Scotland at the 1986 World Cup?

12

Which two players head the list of Scottish goalscorers?

FOOTBALL: HOME
ALL ROUNDERS

1

Which keeper represented Scotland at both soccer and cricket?

2

For which football club did cricketer Denis Compton play?

3

Which English cricketer played for Scunthorpe United?

4

Who was the last person to play both football and cricket for England?

5

Which England substitute played for Wales in a wartime international?

6

Which long-jump world record holder played football and cricket
for England?

7

Which Manchester City captain once beat Charlie Chaplin at table tennis?

8

What feat was perfomed by Chris Balderstone in September 1975?

9

Which first-class footballer and cricketer went on to manufacture
footballs?

10

Which Welsh international made his film debut in 1998?

11

Which England footballer was filmed sleeping naked?

12

Which England manager co-wrote a series of bestselling detective novels?

FOOTBALL: HOME
QUOTES: WHO SAID...? (2)

1

"I don't know much about football. I know what a goal is."

2

"There are no bungs in football, only presents."

3

"Show me a player who's thick and I'll show you a player who
has problems."

4

"Football's a difficult business, and aren't they prima donnas?"

5

"Football is about glory ...about going out and beating the lot."

6

"Some think football is a matter of life and death. It's much more
serious than that."

7

"Stick it up your bollocks!"

8

[Of Ryan Giggs] "He could play in a telephone box and still find the door."

9

"Italians have a very closed life. Football is all their life is."

10

[On Michael Owen] "He's got the legs of a salmon."

11

"I didn't say them things I said."

12

"I can see the carrot at the end of the tunnel."

FOOTBALL: HOME
ODDITIES (2)

1

Which team do the Chuckle Brothers support?

2

Which 1970s Arsenal star cut off his big toe with a lawnmower?

3

Which clubs did Robert Maxwell want to merge into
Thames Valley Royals?

4

Who was the first British footballer to join a Portuguese club?

5

Of 12 original Football League clubs, which is no longer a member?

6

With which club did Frank Swift spend his entire career?

7

Whose frozen ground was opened as an ice rink in 1963?

8

Who has kept most clean sheets in a Premiership season?

9

Which future prime minister sold programmes at Raith Rovers?

10

Who were the only unbeaten team in the 1974 World Cup finals?

11

Which Scottish club is named after an English rugby team?

12

Which is the only English league side whose letters cannot be filled in?

FOOTBALL: HOME
WHERE DO THEY PLAY?

1

Who plays at the Galpharm Stadium?

2

What is Dundee United's home ground?

3

Which club's former address was Cold Blow Lane?

4

Which Northern Ireland club play at Mourneview Park?

5

Which Scottish Club play at Ochilview Park?

6

Which English club plays at Carrow Road?

7

Where do Derry City play?

8

What is the name of Wrexham's ground?

9

At which Scottish League ground is the Cemetery End?

10

Which English league club's ground was bombed in World War I?

11

Where do Dunfermline Athletic play?

12

Which team play at the Crabbie Athletic ground?

FOOTBALL: HOME
MANAGERS

1

In which year did Don Revie suddenly quit his England job?

2

Which club did Norman Hunter manage from 1985 to 1987?

3

In which year did Ally MacLeod become Scotland manager?

4

When did Jimmy Hill quit as Coventry manager?

5

Which England World Cup winner became Southend manager in 1984?

6

Which Lancashire club had just two managers between 1970 and 1994?

7

Who was England manager immediately before Alf Ramsey?

8

Who was appointed Scotland's temporary manager in 1958?

9

Who was the shortest-serving manager in the English league?

10

Which manager took his club to most League Cup wins?·

11

Which Lincoln City manager resigned to join a US religious sect?

12

Which Portuguese club did Tommy Docherty manage?

FOOTBALL: HOME
ANCIENT HISTORY

....

1

When was the Football Association formed?

....

2

Which Frenchman was the force behind the creation of the World Cup?

....

3

Which ancient people played a kind of football called "harpastum"?

....

4

Which English king banned football in 1363?

....

5

In which Italian city was the game of "calcio storico" played in the
16th-century?

....

6

Which is the oldest football competition, founded in 1871?

....

7

On which Scottish island is the medieval "Ba Game" still played
at Hogmanay?

....

8

In which year was the Spanish Liga founded?

....

9

What did the FA ban in 1921?

....

10

Who founded the Argentinian Football Association in 1893?

....

11

Which South American national sides were the first to play each other?

....

12

Which was the first African country to play an international match?

....

1

Who is the only professional player to win a "golden set"?

2

Who won the shortest ever Grand Slam final?

3

What was the longest tennis match ever (in time)?

4

Who has won the most men's titles in the open era (since 1968)?

5

Who has won the most singles titles?

6

How many successive years did Roger Federer top the world rankings?

7

In which year was Jennifer Capriati joint women's number one?

8

Who had the highest percentage of wins in his Grand Slam career?

9

Who won most major singles titles before the open era?

10

Which woman recorded the longest match-winning streak?

11

Who was the first Wimbledon women's champion?

12

Who played most men's matches at Wimbledon?

26
TENNIS
NICKNAMES: WHO WERE...?

. . . .

1

"The Bounding Basque"

. . . .

2

"Little Mo"

. . . .

3

"Rocket"

. . . .

4

"Pancho"

. . . .

5

"The Flying Dutchman"

. . . .

6

"Peaches"

. . . .

7

"Rabbit"

. . . .

8

"Old Crankshaft"

. . . .

9

"Wheels"

. . . .

10

"Scud"

. . . .

11

"Gorgeous Gussie"

. . . .

12

"Little Miss Poker Face"

. . . .

TENNIS
NAME THE CITY: WHERE ARE...?

1

The Arthur Ashe Stadium

2

Qizhong Forest Sports City

3

The Rod Laver Arena

4

Court Philippe Chatrier

5

The IMPACT Arena

6

The Hallenstadion

7

The Hisense Arena

8

The Netaji Indoor Stadium

9

The Stade Uniprix

10

Queen's Club

11

Dom Sportova

12

Sportpaleis Merksem

1

In medieval tennis, what was used to strike the ball?

2

Which early form of tennis was played by French kings?

3

In which play does Shakespeare mention "tennis balls"?

4

In which revolution was the Tennis Court Oath a significant event?

5

In which year did Walter Wingfield devise the modern game of tennis?

6

How did the term "love" originate?

7

What was the original game played by the All England Tennis Club?

8

Who introduced tennis to the USA in 1874?

9

In which year were the first US Open Championships held?

10

In which year was the Australian Open first played?

11

Which two teams played in the first Davis Cup tournament in 1900?

12

Which major tennis organization was formed in 1913?

TENNIS
TECHNICAL TERMS

1

What is a "golden set"?

2

Which side is the deuce court?

3

What is "a bagel job"?

4

What is a "wood shot"?

5

Who was the most famous exponent of the "slamdunk smash"?

6

Where is the alley?

7

What is a "get"?

8

What is a "flat"?

9

What is a kick serve?

10

What is the I-Formation?

11

What does WTA stand for?

12

How is a "jamming shot" hit?

1

[Of tennis] "Violent action in an atmosphere of total tranquility."

2

"It's one-on-one out there, man. There ain't no hiding."

3

"I was never that bright at school so I had to be clever with something."

4

"You have to be a killer. But it's important not to lose your appearance."

5

"One has to know how to lose with humility."

6

"I will die without having played enough tennis."

7

"I am retiring from tennis – I do not want to put myself through all this."

8

"What a polite game tennis is."

9

"Anybody on for a game of tennis?"

10

"We both play with the same ball, but one of us places it better."

11

"First to the net, first to the pub."

12

"Good shot, bad luck, and hell are the basic words used in a game of tennis."

TENNIS
THE GRAND SLAM

1

Which are the four Grand Slam tournaments?

2

In which year did Donald Budge complete the first Grand Slam?

3

Who is the only player to have won two singles Grand Slams?

4

In which years?

5

Which is the first Grand Slam tournament in the calendar year?

6

What is the playing surface in the French Open?

7

What was included in Steffi Graf's "Golden Slam" of 1988?

8

How many singles players have won a Grand Slam?

9

Which Grand Slam event is played on Decoturf?

10

What is the term for winning three out of the four tournaments?

11

Who are the only men's doubles team to complete a Grand Slam?

12

What is unique about Margaret Court's Grand Slam record?

TENNIS
THE DAVIS CUP

1

Which country has won the Davis Cup most times?

2

Who founded the competition?

3

Who handed South Africa walkover victory in 1974?

4

Who is the youngest player ever to appear?

5

Who has played the most Davis Cup rubbers?

6

In which year did France first win the Cup?

7

How many rubbers are there in a Cup tie?

8

How many teams are in the World Group of the Davis Cup?

9

How many teams in total competed in 2007?

10

Are Davis Cup rubbers three or five sets?

11

Which country recorded its first and only Cup triumph in 1976?

12

When was the last time Great Britain won the Davis Cup?

TENNIS
RECORD BREAKERS (2)

1

Who sent down the fastest recorded serve?

2

Who was the youngest women's champion at Wimbledon?

3

Who has won most titles in the Australian Open?

4

When was the first Women's World Real Tennis championships held?

5

Which tennis tournament has attracted the most competitors?

6

Who was the oldest Wimbledon men's champion?

7

How long was the longest ever doubles match?

8

Who has recorded the fastest women's serve?

9

What is the world's longest tennis rally?

10

Who sent down the greatest number of aces in a Grand Slam match?

11

Who has won most doubles titles at a single tournament?

12

Who is the only English king to have played at Wimbledon?

TENNIS
NAME THE YEAR

1

In which year did the French championships let in foreign players?

2

When did Margaret Dupont first become US women's champion?

3

In which year did Goran Ivanisevic win Wimbledon?

4

When did Maria Sharapova win the US Open?

5

When were the first Australian Open Championships?

6

In which two years was Ken Rosewall Australian champion?

7

When did Croatia win the Davis Cup?

8

In which year was tennis dropped from the Olympic Games?

9

When was it reinstated?

10

In which year did Margaret Court win the Grand Slam?

11

When did the first non-Briton win a Wimbledon title?

12

In which year did the "Woodies" win their last Wimbledon doubles title?

TENNIS
WIMBLEDON (1)

1

When did Norman Brookes become the first foreign men's singles champion?

2

Since then, how many Britons have won the men's title?

3

And how many Britons have won the women's title?

4

In which year did five bombs fall on Centre Court?

5

Who was the first black winner of a Wimbledon title?

6

In which year were the first "open" championships?

7

What unique events occurred in 1973?

8

Who won the men's title that year?

9

Who was the first German to win the men's singles?

10

Whose record did Roger Federer equal in 2007?

11

When was the centenary of the women's singles championship?

12

But – in which year was the 100th women's singles championship?

TENNIS
WIMBLEDON (2)

1

Why did Andre Agassi and Steffi Graf appear on Centre Court in May 2009?

2

How many junior events take place at the Championships?

3

What significant rule about previous winners was changed in 1922?

4

How many match courts are there at Wimbledon?

5

What are the BBGs?

6

How much prize money did a singles champion receive in 2009?

7

Who has won most men's doubles titles at Wimbledon?

8

Who won most consecutive women's singles titles before the Open Era?

9

Who is the lowest-ranked man to have won a singles title?

10

Which was the longest singles final ever?

11

Who has played most matches at Wimbledon?

12

Who won the girls' singles title in 2008?

1

What is the full name of the venue for the US Open?

2

How do US Open rules differ from those of other Grand Slam tournaments?

3

In which state was the first women's championship played in 1887?

4

What is the prize money for US singles champions?

5

Who has won most men's titles?

6

Who is the youngest person to win a singles title?

7

Who was the men's runner-up in 2008?

8

How many times was Ken Rosewall US men's champion?

9

Who was the first ever women's champion?

10

How many Brazilians have won US Open titles?

11

Which pair won the mixed doubles title in 2008?

12

Who has won most women's singles titles in the Open Era?

TENNIS
THE FRENCH OPEN

....

1

Who was Roland Garros?

....

2

When were the French championships opened to overseas players?

....

3

How many times has Roger Federer won the French Open?

....

4

Who was the first open era man to win both Wimbledon and the French Open?

....

5

Who has won most French titles altogether?

....

6

Who won most consecutive women's titles?

....

7

Who is the youngest player to win the men's singles?

....

8

What feat was performed by Margaret Scriven in 1933?

....

9

Who won the women's doubles in 2009?

....

10

Who was the first ever men's champion?

....

11

In what year did he triumph?

....

12

Who was the women's runner-up in 2009?

....

1

Until which year was the Australian Open played on grass?

2

What did the Williams sisters uniquely achieve in 2009?

3

What is the new court surface at Melbourne Park?

4

When were the Australian Championships last played in New Zealand?

5

What was the original name of Melbourne Park?

6

How many times did Jack Kramer play in the Championships?

7

Why was there no tournament in 1986?

8

Who has won the most Australian women's singles titles?

9

Who has won the most men's singles and doubles titles?

10

Who was the youngest winner of the men's singles?

11

And who was the oldest?

12

Who was the women's runner-up in 2009?

....

1

Lenglen beat Wills in France.

....

2

Gibson beat Hard at Forest Hills.

....

3

Borg beat McEnroe at Wimbledon.

....

4

Gonzalez beat Pasarell at Wimbledon.

....

5

Cochet beat Tilden at Wimbledon.

....

6

Budge beat von Cramm in the Davis Cup.

....

7

Bueno beat Smith at Wimbledon.

....

8

Nadal beat Federer at Wimbledon.

....

9

Ashe beat Connors at Wimbledon.

....

10

Wilander beat Cash in the Australian Open.

....

11

Chang beat Edberg in the French Open.

....

12

Ivanisevic beat Rafter at Wimbledon.

....

1

Which player won six consecutive Grand Slam titles in 1937-8?

2

Which great champion was known as "Big Bill"?

3

Which No. 1 player went on to form the Association of Tennis Professionals?

4

Which brilliant left-hander was born in Rockhampton, Queensland?

5

How old was Pancho Gonzalez when he played Charlie Pasarell at Wimbledon?

6

What is Bjorn Borg's record for consecutive singles wins at Wimbledon?

7

Who were "The Four Musketeers"?

8

Who equalled Sampras's record of 14 major titles in June 2009?

9

How many years was Fred Perry rated World No. 1?

10

How old was Boris Becker when he first won a Wimbledon title?

11

Who lost to Borg at Wimbledon 1980, only to beat him in the US Open?

12

Who won 81 straight games on clay courts between 2005 and 2007?

TENNIS
FAMOUS PLAYERS – WOMEN

1

Who was ranked World No.1 for 377 consecutive weeks?

2

Who became the first Australian Aboriginal tennis star in the 1970s?

3

Which player was known as "La Divine" by the French press?

4

What (then) unique feat did Maureen Connolly perform in 1953?

5

Who was the first Australian woman to win a Wimbledon singles title?

6

What did Charlie Chaplin call "the most beautiful sight he'd ever seen"?

7

In which country was Martina Navratilova born?

8

Who beat Bobby Riggs in the "Battle of the Sexes" in 1973?

9

Who gave her name to the Cup challenge between US and British women?

10

Who was singles champion in Wimbledon's centenary year?

11

Whom did Martina Navratilova call "the female Federer"?

12

Who has the highest percentage of victories of any professional player?

1

Was tennis included at the inaugural Games of 1896?

2

In which year was tennis dropped from the Olympics?

3

When did it return?

4

Which country has won most tennis medals in all?

5

How many medals has India won?

6

Which player has won the most Olympic medals?

7

From which country did all the 2008 women's singles medallists come?

8

At which Games were world ranking points first given to competitors?

9

In which city was the 2008 tennis tournament held?

10

Who won gold in the 2008 women's doubles?

11

Which medal was won by Novak Djokovic?

12

Which country has won the most gold medals in tennis?

TENNIS
WHO WAS THE MOST FAMOUS PARTNER OF...?

....

1

Frew McMillan

....

2

Todd Woodbridge

....

3

Paul McNamee

....

4

Jamie Murray

....

5

Martina Navratilova

....

6

Rosie Casals

....

7

Tony Roche

....

8

Helena Sukova

....

9

Fred Stolle

....

10

Ken McGregor

....

11

Venus Williams

....

12

Peter Fleming

....

1

What is the smallest winning margin in the Tour de France?

2

In which year was the first pedal cycle built?

3

Which city hosted the first recorded cycle race?

4

Which country popularized the type of road race called a *kermesse*?

5

In which year was the first Road Racing World Championship?

6

When was the first Tour de France staged?

7

And who was the first winner?

8

What kind of race is a Madison?

9

Whose streamlined machine helped him to 4,000m gold in the 1992 Olympics?

10

Who holds the world track record for one kilometre?

11

Whose nickname was "Le Cannibale"?

12

What is the name of Spain's premier road race?

RACING & SPEED
CYCLING (2)

1

What name is given to short circuit road races, often in city centres?

2

What is the non-stop, single-stage, race from coast to coast of the USA?

3

Which big-eared rider was known as "Il Elefantino"?

4

When did Lance Armstrong win the last of his seven Tours de France?

5

What is the destination of the French race known as
"the Hell of the North"?

6

In which year was cycling first included in the Olympic Games?

7

Which major road race is held in Flanders every spring?

8

Which Australian city stages the Tour Down Under?

9

And who was the winner in 2009?

10

Which country has won most cycling golds at the Olympics?

11

Who won the women's road race at the 2008 Olympics?

12

How many cycling medals overall did Britain win at the
Beijing Olympics?

1

Which 1913 Tour rider was penalized for helping a blacksmith mend his bike?

2

Which rider was known (in French) as "The Badger"?

3

What kind of race do the French call "contre-la-montre"?

4

What is "a granny gear"?

5

Which event at the 2008 Olympics was won by Julien Absalon?

6

Which country hosted the 2009 UCI Track Cycling World Championships?

7

And which team won the most medals there?

8

Whose nickname was "Super Mario"?

9

What kind of cycle race is a "keirin"?

10

Who won the men's keirin at the 2008 Olympics?

11

Which title at the Beijing Olympics was won by Victoria Pendleton?

12

Who holds the men's record for longest distance cycled in one hour on any bike?

RACING & SPEED
CYCLING (4)

1

Which rider's nickname was "Big Mig"?

2

What is a bidon?

3

Who holds the men's one-hour record on a conventional bike?

4

Who won the Tour de France in 2008?

5

When was the King of the Mountains competition added to the Tour?

6

Who has been King of the Mountains on most occasions?

7

Who was the first rider to win the Tour de France five times?

8

How many races were won by Eddy Merckx in his career?

9

Who won the French Women's Championship 11 consecutive times?

10

When is a rider "on the rivet"?

11.

Who was known as "The Tashkent Terror"?

12

Which city hosted the 2008 World Cycling Championships?

1

Where was the first proper race course established in North America?

....

2

And in which year was it founded?

....

3

In which city is the street race called "Il Palio"?

....

4

Which was the first race course in Britain?

....

5

How many flat races make up the English Classics?

....

6

Which horse first achieved the Triple Crown of British wins in 1953?

....

7

Which race, with the Derby and St Leger, makes up that Triple?

....

8

Which Derby winner holds the record for the biggest margin of victory?

....

9

In which year was the first Melbourne Cup?

....

10

At what odds did Frankie Dettori win all seven races in a day at Ascot?

....

11

Which jockey won the first ever Grand National?

....

12

Who was Champion National Hunt jockey from 1995 to 2009?

....

1

What is a "bumper race"?

2

Which race horse was famously given two bottles of Guinness a day?

3

Which two jockeys tied as Champion flat racers in 2007?

4

Which is the only horse to have won the Grand National three times?

5

What is the greatest number of horses starting a Grand National?

6

Which horse holds the speed record over one mile?

7

Which was the last horse to win the US Triple Crown?

8

Which race, with the Kentucky Derby and Belmont Stakes, makes up that Triple?

9

In which Irish county is the Irish Derby run?

10

Who rode Nijinsky to his UK Triple Crown in 1970?

11

In which country is the Canterbury Park Racecourse?

12

Who said (at Aintree) "How dreadful water tastes without the benefit of whisky"?

1

What landmark was reached by Tony McCoy in February 2009?

2

What, in betting slang, is a "Bismarck"?

3

Which legendary US jockey rode an astonishing 8,833 winners?

4

Which horse won 5 consecutive Cheltenham Gold Cups?

5

Who is the only English monarch to have owned a
Grand National winner?

6

What is the maximum number of horses now allowed to start a
Grand National?

7

Who rode Alleged to consecutive Prix de L'Arc de Triomphe victories?

8

In which country is the Nakayama Racecourse?

9

Which was the last horse to win the Irish Triple Crown?

10

At which US course is the Mother Goose Stakes run?

11

Who is the first woman to have trained a Grand National winner?

12

Which trainer won 16 English and 27 Irish classic races?

1

How many times was Gordon Richards Champion Jockey?

2

What odds are known as "Burlington Bertie"?

3

In which year was the first China Speed Horse Race?

4

Which race offers the largest purse in the world?

5

Which horse holds the world speed record over a distance of 2 miles?

6

Which horse won the first Cheltenham Gold Cup in 1924?

7

In which year did only two horses finish the Grand National?

8

How many mares have won the Grand National?

9

Which US race is known as "The Run for the Roses"?

10

What distance is The Derby?

11

In which year did Mill Reef win the Derby?

12

Which is the only horse to win Welsh, Scottish and English Nationals?

RACING & SPEED
SWIMMING (1)

1

At which Olympics did Mark Spitz win his seven swimming golds?

2

Which two Olympic champions went on to play Tarzan on film?

3

Who holds the men's record for the 50m freestyle?

4

Who holds the greatest number of women's world records?

5

What length is a standard long-course pool?

6

In which year was the front crawl introduced to Britain?

7

Who was the first person to swim the English Channel?

8

Who won the Men's 100m at the 1896 Olympics?

9

When did the first women's swimming races appear in the Olympics?

10

What, in diving, is a "rip"?

11

Which woman won 100m freestyle gold at 3 Olympics back-to-back?

12

Who was the first woman to swim the English Channel?

1

Who is the record holder for the men's 100m and 200m breaststroke?

2

What kind of race is "IM" short for?

3

Which long-armed swimmer was nicknamed "The Albatross"?

4

Who won the women's 800m freestyle at the 2008 Olympics?

5

In synchronized swimming, what is a "flamingo"?

6

How many Olympic diving golds have Britain won?

7

In which year was the first World Cup held?

8

Which woman has won the most swimming golds at a single Olympics?

9

How long did Benoît Lecomte take to swim the Atlantic in 1998?

10

Which country has won the most Olympic swimming golds overall?

11

In which year were Olympic swimming events held in the River Seine?

12

In which city is the Ying Tung Natatorium?

1

In which year were goggles first used at the Olympics?

2

How many world records are held by Australia's Grant Hackett?

3

What nationality is the record-breaking swimmer Kirsty Coventry?

4

In which year was the butterfly stroke first allowed at the Olympics?

5

What strange kind of swimming race was staged at the 1900 Games?

6

Who won the men's 100m backstroke at the Beijing Olympics?

7

What nickname was given to Eric Moussambani at the 2000 Olympics?

8

Which swimming stroke was pioneered by Arthur Trudgen?

9

What became known as a "Berkoff Blastoff"?

10

Which Dutch swimmer won three women's golds at the 2000 Games?

11

Which Australian multi-record holder retired before her 17th birthday?

12

Which city will host the World Aquatics Championships in 2011?

1

In which year did the first organized motor race take place?

2

How many competitors showed up for this race?

3

Which pioneering motor race club was founded in 1895?

4

In which year was the first Grand Prix held at Le Mans?

5

Who was the first winner of the Formula One drivers' championship?

6

In which year did he win?

7

What is a T-car?

8

Who pushed his car over the finish line to win the 1959 championship?

9

Who was the last British driver to win the Le Mans 24-Hour Race?

10

What is the tightest ever winning margin in an Indy 500 race?

11

Who is the only driver to record seven Le Mans 24-Hour victories?

12

How many Grand Prix wins were recorded by Michael Schumacher?

1

In which country was the V8 Supercars race category developed?

2

What kind of cars are involved in NASCAR races?

3

In which year were the first World Rally Championships held?

4

What make of car did Alberto Ascari drive for most of his career?

5

On which track did Niki Lauda suffer his horrific accident in 1976?

6

Which great British driver won 16 Grand Prix races but never the championship?

7

Which driver was nicknamed "The Professor"?

8

Who was driver's champion for four consecutive years from 1954?

9

What is the meaning of a red- and yellow-striped flag?

10

Who was the World Rally Champion driver in 2008?

11

At which Grand Prix was grid position first determined by qualifying times?

12

Which two makes of car were sponsored by the Nazis in the 1930s?

RACING & SPEED
MOTOR RACING (3)

. . . .

1

In which year was Formula One created?

. . . .

2

At which track was the first F1 championship race staged?

. . . .

3

Which country will stage its first F1 Grand Prix in 2011?

. . . .

4

Which car won the first F1 Constructors' Championships in 1958?

. . . .

5

When did the Williams team first become Constructors' Champions?

. . . .

6

Which driver was nicknamed "Baby Face"?

. . . .

7

Who starred in the 1971 film *Le Mans*?

. . . .

8

Which Briton was F1 champion in 1963 and 1965?

. . . .

9

What is the lowest number of cars to finish a Grand Prix?

. . . .

10

Who won the 2009 Indianapolis 500 race?

. . . .

11

Which F1 driver is known as "Jimmy Savile"?

. . . .

12

Which Indy 500 winner asked for a glass of milk in 1933,
starting a tradition?

. . . .

RACING & SPEED
MOTORCYCLING

1

When were the first Isle of Man TT races?

2

Which country won the first speedway World Cup?

3

Which motorcycling champion went on to win a Formula One title?

4

Which New Zealander was speedway Champion six times in the 1970s?

5

In motocross, what is a "washboard"?

6

Who was 500cc World Champion from 2001 to 2005?

7

What is the maximum capacity allowed for a superbike engine?

8

Who was the 2008 Superbike World Champion?

9

Which motorcycling title did Giacomo Agostini win a record 8 times?

10

For which two teams did Barry Sheene ride?

11

What kind of vehicles are used in snowcross races?

12

What was the venue of the first Speedway World Championship in 1936?

RACING & SPEED
ROWING

1

What is the world's oldest known regular rowing contest?

2

In which year was the first University Boat Race?

3

What is a "skeg"?

4

At which Games did Steve Redgrave win his first Olympic gold?

5

On which lake will the 2011 World Rowing Championships take place?

6

Which country won most medals at the 2008 World Championships?

7

Why were there no rowing events at the 1896 Olympics?

8

Which rower has won the most Olympic medals?

9

Who won gold in men's single sculls at the 2008 Olympics?

10

In which rowing events did Britain win gold at Beijing?

11

What is the word "cox" short for?

12

Which famous child psychologist won rowing gold in the
1924 Olympics?

RACING & SPEED
SAILING

1

In which year was the first America's Cup?

2

What kind of race is a "round-the-cans"?

3

Who set a record for the fastest solo world circumnavigation in 2005?

4

Who was the first person to sail solo round the world from east to west?

5

Which was the first non-USA boat to win the America's Cup?

6

In which year did that shock result take place?

7

What kind of sailing craft is an Yngling?

8

Who won the 2008 Vendee Globe solo round-the-world race?

9

Who was the first person to sail non-stop and solo round the world?

10

Which prime minister captained the winning team in the 1971 Admiral's Cup?

11

What (to the nearest day) is the solo round-the-world speed record?

12

How long was the smallest boat to sail round the world?

RACING & SPEED
EQUESTRIAN

1

What was showjumping first known as in the 1860s?

2

How many faults or penalties are incurred for a refusal at a jump?

3

Where will the World Equestrian Games take place in 2010?

4

Which rider became the first competitor to appear in 8 Olympics?

5

What kind of event is a "puissance"?

6

Which country has won most golds at the World Equestrian Games?

7

Which Briton won the 1982 Eventing World Championship
on Regal Realm?

8

Which city hosted the 2006 Showjumping World Championships?

9

In dressage, what is a "piaffe"?

10

What are the three equestrian disciplines at an Olympic Games?

11

What did all Olympic equestrian competitors have to be until 1952?

12

Where were the equestrian events held at the 2008 Olympics?

RACING & SPEED
SKIING

1

In ski-jumping, where is the "K point"?

2

In which year was downhill racing first included in the Olympics?

3

Who won the women's slalom gold at the 2006 Winter Olympics?

4

In which year did Franz Klammer retire?

5

Which Belgian skier won 12 women's world titles in the 1930s?

6

What are the two criteria on which ski-jumpers are judged?

7

What caused the cancellation of the 1995 World Skiing Championships?

8

What is the speed record for downhill skiing?

9

Who won gold in the men's Alpine Downhill at the 2006
Winter Olympics?

10

Which city hosted the 2006 Winter Olympics?

11

What three skiing runs are included in the Combined Event?

12

Which city has been chosen to stage the 2014 Winter Olympics?

1

Which hot-air ballooning trophy is named after a US newspaper tycoon?

2

A bobsleigh team from which unlikely island lit up the 1988 Winter Olympics?

3

In canoeing, what is a "Telemark turn"?

4

What kind of racing car burns fuel at about 1.5 gallons (6 litres) a second?

5

In which sport was Mick the Miller the most celebrated racer?

6

Which Hollywood actress won 10 consecutive World Skating Championships?

7

What is the meaning of the French word *luge*?

8

Who won the Men's Downhill 2008 World Mountain Bike Championships?

9

In which country were the first Mountaineering World Championships held in 2001?

10

What is the fastest non-motorized sport without land contact?

11

What is the name of the most famous dog sled race, set in Alaska?

12

In which year was windsurfing added to the Olympic sailing events?

RUGBY UNION
RECORD BREAKERS

1

Who has scored the most tries in internationals?

2

Who is the leading try scorer for New Zealand?

3

Who has scored the most international points for Australia?

4

Who has scored the most tries in a Six Nations match?

5

What is the highest score by one side in the Six Nations?

6

Who is the highest points scorer ever in internationals?

7

What is the fastest test try ever scored?

8

What world record is held by Derek Bevan?

9

Which sides took part in the first ever international in 1871?

10

Which player has made most appearances in the World Cup?

11

Who scored the most drop goals in a single World Cup game?

12

Who has scored most World Cup tries?

RUGBY UNION
NICKNAMES – WHICH TEAMS ARE KNOWN AS...?

1

"The All Whites"

2

"Los Teros"

3

"The Naki"

4

"The Tigers"

5

"The Sea Eagles"

6

"The Canucks"

7

"The Cherry Blossoms"

8

"Streeptruie"

9

"Bokke"

10

"The Black Ferns"

11

"The Cherry and Whites"

12

"The Exiles"

1

Where is a box kick aimed?

2

What is a garryowen?

3

Which side of a scrum is the loosehead prop?

4

What is "truck and trailer" – and is it legal?

5

Who are the "uglies"?

6

What happens during the third half?

7

What is the meaning of "ping"?

8

Who are the "girls"?

9

What happens during "handbags"?

10

What position is a first five-eighth?

11

Which backs are involved in ten-man rugby along with the pack?

12

Which players are the tight five?

1

At which English public school was rugby probably invented?

2

Which schoolboy gave his name to the World Cup trophy?

3

Which was the first rugby club, founded in 1843?

4

In which year was the Rugby Football Union founded?

5

Who captained England in their first ever international?

6

How much was a try originally worth?

7

What law regarding the ball was introduced in 1892?

8

In which year did the northern clubs split from the RFU?

9

Which team won rugby gold at the 1920 Olympics?

10

In which year was rugby dropped from the Olympic Games?

11

Between which two countries is the Bledisloe Cup played?

12

In which year did the Five Nations competition resume after
World War Two?

1

Which English team plays at The Rec?

2

What is the name of Gloucester's ground?

3

In which city is the Stadio Flaminio?

4

Which country plays at the Millennium Stadium?

5

What is the name of the Harlequins' ground?

6

In which city is the Croke Park ground?

7

In which city is Stadium Australia?

8

What is the proper name of the NZ ground known as
"The House of Pain"?

9

What is the main rugby venue in Cape Town?

10

What is the name of France's main international ground?

11

Which country plays tests at Velez Sarsfield?

12

In which year was Scotland's Murrayfield first opened?

1

"You've got to get your first tackle in early, even if it's late."

2

"I prefer rugby to soccer. I enjoy the violence in rugby." [A film star]

3

"You don't need 57 old farts running rugby."

4

"If you can't take a punch, you should play table tennis."

5

"Subdue and penetrate."

6

"My favourite sport at school was rugby. Rugby is about teamwork."

7

"Nobody ever beats Wales at rugby, they just score more points."

8

[On England's World Cup win] "The best team in the world by one minute."

9

"Rugby is a beastly game played by gentlemen."

10

"Bill, there's a guy just run on the park with your backside on his chest."

11

[Of Jonah Lomu] "There's no doubt about it, he's a big bastard."

12

"The whole point of rugby is that it is a state of mind, a spirit."

1

When, according to legend, did William Webb Ellis pick up the ball?

2

In which year was the first World Cup?

3

In which year were the rules of rugby football first published?

4

When was the Tri-Nations Championship established?

5

When did Scotland last win the Six Nations?

6

When was Gareth Edwards's famous Barbarians' try against
the All Blacks?

7

In which year did Bath win the Heineken Cup?

8

Which was the year of Gareth Edwards's first cap for Wales?

9

After which World Cup did Michael Lynagh retire?

10

When was the value of a drop goal reduced from four points to three?

11

In which year did rugby union become professional?

12

When did the Five Nations become Six?

1

Which country has won the most Home Grand Slams?

2

Which is the oldest two-nation competition with the Six Nations?

3

What is the trophy contested by France and Italy?

4

In the Six Nations, which is "the invisible cup"?

5

When did France first win the championship outright?

6

When did England last win a Grand Slam?

7

Who has played in most Six (or Five) Nations matches?

8

Who scored most tries in his Five Nations career?

9

Which nation scored most points in a season?

10

Which two teams have won most victories since 2000?

11

Which pair were the top try scorers of the 2009 competition?

12

And who was the top points scorer?

RUGBY UNION
THE TRI-NATIONS

1

In which year did Australia and New Zealand first play each other?

2

Which team won the Tri-Nations for the first time in 2000?

3

Which countries take part in the Pacific Tri-Nations?

4

Whose last-gasp try for the All Blacks won the opening game in 2000?

5

Who is the top try scorer in the Tri-Nations?

6

Who has scored most Tri-Nations points for South Africa?

7

How many matches have been drawn (to 2009)?

8

Which country is often rumoured as the next to join the Tri-Nations?

9

How many points are awarded for a win?

10

How many tries must a side score to earn a bonus point?

11

In which year did South Africa first tour Australia and New Zealand?

12

How many matches were played in the 2009 series?

1

How many nations take part in the World Cup finals?

2

Which countries hosted the first World Cup in 1987?

3

How many Asian teams took part in the first World Cup?

4

Whose extra-time drop goal won the Cup for South Africa in 1995?

5

Who were the first nation to win the World Cup twice?

6

How far did Argentina progress in the 2007 Cup?

7

How many matches were played at the 2007 finals?

8

Who will host the 2011 World Cup?

9

Who has scored most points in one competition?

10

What is the biggest winning margin in a qualifier?

11

Who is the oldest player to appear in a World Cup Final?

12

Who is the only player to have scored points in two World Cup Finals?

. . . .

1

In which year did the All Blacks make their first Northern
Hemisphere tour?

. . . .

2

In which year did they first beat the Springboks in a series?

. . . .

3

What motif decorates an All Black shirt?

. . . .

4

What was composed by Te Rauparaha?

. . . .

5

What nickname was given to the unbeaten 1924 touring side?

. . . .

6

What is New Zealand's longest winning streak?

. . . .

7

Who knocked the All Blacks out of the 2007 World Cup?

. . . .

8

What was the nickname of lock Colin Meads?

. . . .

9

Who is the most capped All Black?

. . . .

10

Who is the youngest player to appear in an All Black jersey?

. . . .

11

Who has scored most international points for New Zealand?

. . . .

12

What record was set by Joe Rokocoko in 2003?

. . . .

RUGBY UNION
THE BRITISH AND IRISH LIONS

1

What was the destination of the first official Home unions tour in 1910?

2

In which year did the Lions first tour Argentina?

3

Who captained the Lions on their 1959 tour of New Zealand?

4

Who coached the victorious 1971 Lions in New Zealand?

5

When did the Lions last win a series against Australia?

6

Which tour to South Africa featured the infamous "99 call"?

7

Who was the Lions captain on that tour?

8

Why did the Lions play a one-off match against France in 1989?

9

What is the highest score posted against New Zealand?

10

Against which side have the Lions played most tests?

11

Which country will the Lions tour in 2013?

12

Against which Asian team did the Lions play an unofficial match in 1950?

1

What kind of flower is a Springbok emblem?

2

In which year did South Africa play their first international match?

3

What is the biggest of all Springbok victories?

4

What was the winning scoreline in the 1995 World Cup final?

5

Why had the team missed out on the first two World Cups?

6

Why were two All Blacks dropped from the 1928 South African tour?

7

Whom did the Springboks play in the "Battle of Boet Erasmus stadium"?

8

Which side did the Springboks defeat in the 2007 World Cup Final?

9

Who was the only non-white player in the 1995 World Cup side?

10

Who is the most-capped South African player?

11

Who is the Springboks' record try scorer?

12

Who was South Africa's coach at the 2007 World Cup?

RUGBY UNION
THE WALLABIES

1

How many tries did David Campese score for Australia?

2

How many times have Australia won the World Cup?

3

Who is the most-capped Wallaby?

4

In which year did Australia play its first test against the British Isles?

5

How many times have Australia won the Bledisloe Cup?

6

Which trophy does Australia compete for with England?

7

What is Australia's worst ever international defeat?

8

Which 1990s second row forward was also captain and a place kicker?

9

How many times have the Wallabies won the Tri-Nations?

10

Who was Australia's coach at the 1999 World Cup?

11

At which Olympic Games did Australia win gold?

12

What position did Ken Catchpole play in?

. . . .

1

Which brilliant Welsh full-back was also Wimbledon junior champion?

. . . .

2

What position did Willie John McBride play in?

. . . .

3

How old was Barry John when he retired?

. . . .

4

Who captained South Africa to their 1995 World Cup triumph?

. . . .

5

Who is France's most-capped player?

. . . .

6

Which New Zealand hooker and captain won 63 consecutive caps?

. . . .

7

Which great French full-back was born in Venezuela?

. . . .

8

In which year did David Campese retire?

. . . .

9

Which brilliant Welsh scrum half once held the British pike record?

. . . .

10

Who is England's record try scorer?

. . . .

11

Who was voted New Zealand's "Player of the Century" in 1999?

. . . .

12

Which Russian prince scored two tries on his 1936 England debut?

. . . .

RUGBY LEAGUE
RECORD BREAKERS

1

Who has won the Super League's Man of Steel award most times?

2

Who were the first winners of the Super League?

3

Who scored most tries in a Super League career?

4

Which team has won the Australian Premiership most often?

5

What is the biggest international win by the English team?

6

What is the biggest crowd for a home international in Britain?

7

Who was the first player to convert from rugby union to the league?

8

Who scored most goals in a National Rugby League match?

9

Which country won the first ever World Cup in 1954?

10

Who is the top overall points scorer in the World Cup?

11

Which team has won the World Cup most times?

12

Which club has won the Challenge Cup most times?

81

1

"The Kangaroos"

2

"The Bears"

3

"The Tomahawks"

4

"The Kumuls"

5

"The Cockerels"

6

"The Cedars"

7

"The All Golds"

8

"The Wolfhounds"

9

"The Bati"

10

"The Bravehearts"

11

"Mate Ma'a"

12

"The White Eagles"

RUGBY LEAGUE
TECHNICAL TERMS

1

What is a field goal?

2

What is the function of the dummy half?

3

What is a zero tackle?

4

Where is a behind ball passed?

5

What is a hook line?

6

How does a side overload the ball?

7

What is a voluntary tackle?

8

What is a grubber kick?

9

And what is a banana kick?

10

What is a falcon?

11

What do Australians mean by a hit-up?

12

What is a powerplay?

RUGBY LEAGUE
ANCIENT HISTORY

1

In which year did the Northern clubs break away from the RFU?

2

How many clubs were there in the original league?

3

Which team won the very first Challenge Cup?

4

Which two teams played the first true rugby league international in 1907?

5

When was the first Australian tour of Britain?

6

Which British player drew the first £1000 transfer fee in 1921?

7

Who ordered rugby league to be banned in France in 1941?

8

When was the Rugby League International Federation formed?

9

In which year was the first World Cup?

10

Who captained France in their series victory against Australia in 1951?

11

What temporary but major rule change was made in 1967?

12

When was the first State of Origin match played in Australia?

1

In which English town was Alex Murphy born?

2

Which spindly runner scored a record 796 League tries?

3

Which Aussie captain had his arm broken four times in his career?

4

How many points did Neil Fox score in his career?

5

Which lightning-quick winger had the nickname "Chariots"?

6

Which England scrum half became a rugby union coach for Wales?

7

Which prolific Australian points-scorer was called
"the Bradman of League"?

8

Who was the first non-white player to be selected for a GB tour?

9

Which French player is honoured with a statue outside the
Carcassone ground?

10

Which Australian skipper was awarded the 2000 Golden Boot?

11

Which RU fly half moved to Widnes in 1988, returning to Union in 1995?

12

Which English halfback was nicknamed "Roger the Dodger"?

1

When was the world record for the 800m last broken?

2

What is Hicham El Guerrouj's record for the mile?

3

Who broke the world 150m record in May 2009?

4

Who holds the world 110m hurdles record?

5

Which country holds the 4x100m relay record?

6

Who were the four members of that team?

7

Which record is held by the Czech Jan Zelezny?

8

Who holds the world shot put record?

9

In which year did Michael Johnson last break the 400m record?

10

Which is the oldest of the major track records?

11

Who holds the record for one hour's track running?

12

Who is the current record holder for the high jump?

1

Who holds the record for one mile?

2

Which two records are held by Lornah Kiplagat?

3

How many major records are still held by representatives of the Soviet Union?

4

What is Paul Radcliffe's record time for the marathon?

5

Who holds the world decathlon record?

6

What nationality is high jump record holder Stefka Kostadinova?

7

In which year did Florence Griffith Joyner set her two sprint records?

8

Who holds two world walking records?

9

Which is the oldest of the major track records?

10

Which Chinese athlete holds two middle distance records?

11

Which country's team holds the 4x200m relay record?

12

What is Inessa Kravets's record triple jump distance?

ATHLETICS
NICKNAMES: WHO WAS KNOWN AS...?

....

1

"The Flying Housewife"

....

2

"The Flying Finn"

....

3

"Blade Runner"

....

4

"The Bronze Queen"

....

5

"Pre"

....

6

"G.O.A.T."

....

7

"El Caballo"

....

8

"The Flying Scotsman"

....

9

"Flo-Jo"

....

10

"The Chairman of the Boards"   .

....

11

"The Flying Dutchman"

....

12

"Luz"

....

ATHLETICS
STADIUMS AND TRACKS

1

Which London stadium opened in 1864 on the site of
The Great Exhibition?

2

In which Indian city is the G M C Balayogi Stadium?

3

In which city will the 2011 Pan-American Games be held?

4

When were the Commonwealth Games last held in England?

5

In which Japanese city is the Nagai Stadium?

6

What is the name of the main athletics stadium in Edmonton, Canada?

7

Which city hosted the first IAAF World Championships in 1983?

8

What was the US arena used for the 1987 World Indoor Championships?

9

Which stadium was built to house the 1996 Atlanta Olympics?

10

Which famous feat was performed at the Iffley Road Track?

11

Which English athletics stadium is also known as the "Thunderdome"?

12

In which country is the Fanny Blankers-Koen Stadion?

ATHLETICS
ANCIENT HISTORY

1

In which year were the first Olympics held in Ancient Greece?

2

Which British college claims to be the first to introduce organized athletics?

3

Why is the year 1896 important for athletics?

4

When was the International Association of Athletics Federations formed?

5

Which forerunner of the Commonwealth Games was first staged in 1930?

6

What was most significant about the 1928 Olympics?

7

How many world records did Jesse Owens equal or break in the 1936 Olympics?

8

In which year did Roger Bannister run the first sub-four minute mile?

9

Which was the first regular marathon run outside the Olympics?

10

How many distance golds were won by the "Flying Finns" between 1912 and 1936?

11

In which year were the first Paralympic Games?

12

How many events were included in the first Ancient Olympic games?

1

Which highjump technique was invented by Dick Fosbury?

2

What is the breakline?

3

How many events are there in the heptathlon?

4

Exactly how far is a marathon?

5

What is the scratchline?

6

Where is the plasticine?

7

In which event is the hitch-kick used?

8

What does DNF stand for?

9

What kind of training is fartlek?

10

What is the lead-off leg?

11

What is the power foot?

12

Which activity can be a blind pass or a visual pass?

ATHLETICS
QUOTES: WHO SAID...?

1

"I have always enjoyed going barefoot."

2

"Athletics is a luxury."

3

[Before the London Marathon] "I hope to be the fastest fat old git in the race."

4

"I know I'm no Kim Basinger, but she can't throw a javelin."

5

"I never developed the macho side."

6

"Being a decathlete is like having ten girlfriends."

7

"My country Ethiopia has always won with determination and heroism."

8

[Of his new highjump style] "I never imagined it would revolutionise the event."

9

"I'm for a drug-free sport and always will be."

10

"I don't compete with other discus throwers. I compete with my own history."

11

"I wasn't invited to shake hands with Hitler."

12

"In Cuba we use our champions to promote the sport."

1

In which year was the women's marathon introduced to the Olympics?

2

When was the standard distance of the marathon first fixed?

3

In which year did the first high-jumper clear 7 feet?

4

In which year did Usain Bolt break both 100m and 200m records?

5

When was sprinter Ben Johnson stripped of his Olympic gold?

6

In which year did Jim Thorpe win the Olympic decathlon?

7

In which year was the men's discus record last broken?

8

When did Jim Hines first break 10 seconds for the 100m sprint?

9

In which year's Olympics did Kelly Holmes take two golds?

10

When did Michael Johnson win his first 400m world championship?

11

In which year were the first Paralympics?

12

In which year was the first Ironman Triathlon held?

1
Which forerunner of the Games was founded by
William Brookes in 1850?

2
How many sporting disciplines were included in the 1896 Games?

3
How many rings make up the Olympic symbol?

4
What (in English) is the Olympic motto?

5
In which city is the Olympic flame ignited before every Games?

6
How many countries took part in the 2008 Olympics?

7
Which Olympic official had the idea for the Youth Olympics?

8
Which were the first Olympics to be broadcast on television?

9
Which is the first nation to enter at a Games opening?

10
How much did the opening ceremony for the Beijing Games cost?

11
Whose medals, taken away in 1912, were given back in 1983?

12
Why did Egypt, Iraq and Lebanon boycott the 1956 Olympics?

ATHLETICS
OLYMPIC GAMES (2)

1

Which two US athletes gave a Black Power salute at the 1968 Olympics?

2

What were the alternative Games staged by Communist nations in 1984?

3

What unhappy first was achieved by Hans-Gunnar Liljenwall in 1968?

4

What performance-enhancer was given to the marathon winner in 1904?

5

In which year were eleven Israeli competitors killed by terrorists?

6

What is a modern gold medal made of?

7

Which pair share the record for Olympic golds in athletics?

8

Which two major regions of the world have never hosted a Games?

9

Which city staged the 1900 Games?

10

Which country has hosted the most Summer Olympics?

11

Who won the first ever Olympic marathon in 1896?

12

Which reactionary US official was President of the IOC from 1952-72?

ATHLETICS
OLYMPIC GAMES (3)

1

What is the official number of the 2012 London Games?

2

Which country has competed under its own flag at every modern Games?

3

What defiant act was performed by Stamata Revithi at the 1896 Games?

4

Which city was due to host the (cancelled) Games in 1916?

5

Which company were the very first Olympic sponsors in 1928?

6

In which Games did the Soviet Union team compete for the first time?

7

Which Czech won three long distance golds in 1952?

8

For how many years did Bob Beamon's 1968 longjump record last?

9

Which Romanian gymnast got two perfect scores out of four in 1976?

10

Why did 66 nations boycott the Moscow Games in 1980?

11

What nationality was Eric "The Eel" Moussambani, a celebrity of 2000?

12

Who won his fifth consecutive rowing gold at the Sydney Olympics?

ATHLETICS
OLYMPIC GAMES (4)

1

What was especially astounding about Paavo Nurmi's two golds in 1924?

2

Who won the same two golds in 2004?

3

Where were the (cancelled) 1940 Games due to be held?

4

Which US athlete won three women's sprint golds in 1960?

5

Which two events were won by Lasse Viren in 1972?

6

Which were the most expensive Games in history before 2008?

7

Which major country competed in its first Olympics in 1984?

8

How many long jump gold medals did Carl Lewis win?

9

Which gymnast has won the most gold medals at a single Games?

10

Which year did figure skater John Curry win Gold for Britain?

11

Which event was won by Cathy Freeman at the 2000 Sydney Olympics?

12

Which country gained a shock basketball victory over the USA in 2004?

1

Which marathon runner was attacked by an Irish priest in the 2004 Olympics?

2

Who lost the 1908 marathon after being helped across the line?

3

Which record holder crashed out of the 2004 women's marathon?

4

Which Greek messenger inspired the marathon race?

5

Who holds the present Olympic marathon record?

6

Which country stages the Midnight Sun Marathon?

7

What nationality is Haile Gebrselassie?

8

What marathon record was set by 64 year-old Larry Macon in 2008?

9

In which country does the Man v Horse Marathon take place?

10

Who is the English national record-holder for men's marathons?

11

Who won the first women's marathon at the Olympics in 1984?

12

In which year was the definitive marathon distance decided?

1

In which city did Hicham El Guerrouj set the present 1500m record?

2

Who holds the women's World 1500m record?

3

When did Harold Wilson run the first sub-four minute 1500m?

4

How many metres over 1500 is a metric mile?

5

At which Olympics was the 1500m first run?

6

And who won it?

7

Who has run the most sub-four minute miles?

8

Who was the second person to break the four-minute barrier?

9

Who holds the record for the women's mile?

10

Who holds the UK mile record?

11

Who won the 1500m gold at the 2008 Olympics?

12

What nationality is 1500m women's champion Nancy Jebet Lagat?

1

Who won the women's 100m gold in Beijing?

2

What nationality was record-breaking sprinter Donovan Bailey?

3

Who was the first athlete to win successive Olympic golds in the 100m?

4

What is the record time in the women's 100m?

5

What sprint record is currently held by Maurice Greene?

6

What is the record for the men's 4x100m?

7

Why is 178m a significant distance in the Olympic Games?

8

Where did Michael Johnson set his 400m world record?

9

Who holds the record for the Paralympic 400m?

10

Who is the current women's record holder for the 400m?

11

What is the unique Olympic feat of Alberto Juantorena?

12

Who won Olympic gold in the 2008 women's 400m?

1

Which is the longest standard track event?

2

Who first broke the 13-minute barrier for the 5,000m?

3

What nationality is distance record holder Tirunesh Dibaba?

4

Who is the world record holder for the men's 10,000m?

5

How many world records were set by Ron Clarke?

6

How many laps of an outdoor track is 5,000m?

7

How long is the Great Manchester Run?

8

How many Olympic medals were won by Paavo Nurmi?

9

Who is the only American to win the Olympic 10,000m?

10

Who broke the 29-minute barrier for the 10,000m in 1954?

11

What woman smashed the 10,000m record by an amazing 42 seconds?

12

Which runner collided with Zola Budd in a 1984 Olympic final?

1

What nationality is current high jump record holder Javier Sotomayor?

2

Who has held the women's high jump record since 1987?

3

How do high jump shoes differ from ordinary track shoes?

4

Who holds the British national high jump record?

5

How long was Bob Beamon's famous long jump in 1968?

6

What extra equipment was carried by ancient Greek long jumpers?

7

Who was the first woman to long jump over 7 metres?

8

Who is the current men's long jump record holder?

9

What was different about the triple jump in the 1896 Olympics?

10

What nationality is Nelson Evora, the current triple jump record holder?

11

How were pole vault competitions measured during the 1850s?

12

Who was the first vaulter to clear 6 metres?

1

In international competition, what is the maximum length of a men's javelin?

2

Why was the javelin redesigned in 1986?

3

Which Briton broke the men's world javelin record in 1992?

4

When did Tessa Sanderson win javelin gold at the Olympics?

5

What new style of putting the shot was developed in the early 1970s?

6

Who broke the men's shot record ten times during the 1950s?

7

What is the record shot distance put by a woman?

8

Is the discus part of both ancient and modern forms of pentathlon?

9

Who holds the women's discus record?

10

Who was the first man to throw the discus over 70 metres?

11

What kind of hammer was originally used in the hammer throw?

12

Who holds the current men's hammer record?

ATHLETICS
ALL-ROUNDERS

1

Which long jump world record holder played cricket for England?

2

Which Olympic women's javelin champion went on to become a champion golfer?

3

Which Olympic relay sprinter led a British political party?

4

Which US footballer won two athletics golds at the 1912 Olympics?

5

Which Wimbledon ladies' champion won archery gold at the 1908 Games?

6

Which great middle-distance runner became a British MP in 1992?

7

Which gold medal-winning sprinter also played rugby for Scotland?

8

Which Olympic heptathlete champion played professional basketball?

9

Which great Czech runner took part in the Prague Spring uprising of 1968?

10

Which famous miler became Master of an Oxford college?

11

Which Olympic steeplechaser founded the London Marathon?

12

Which sprint record-holder played for the Dallas Cowboys?

1

What nationality was the great distance runner Lass Viren?

2

Who won the 1500m gold in 1968 despite suffering from gallstones?

3

Who became Mozambique's first Olympic gold medallist in 2000?

4

Which Jamaican sprinter won three golds at the 1970
Commonwealth Games?

5

Which two countries did Wilson Kipketer represent in his career?

6

How old was Daley Thompson when he appeared at the 1976 Olympics?

7

How old was Merlene Ottey when she won a medal at the 2000 Olympics?

8

In which year did Jesse Owens set three world records within an hour?

9

Who wore gold running shoes at the 1996 Olympics?

10

Which Romanian broke the women's high jump record 14 times
in the 1950s?

11

Who was the first man to beat 18m in the triple jump?

12

Who was the first Australian Aboriginal to compete in the Olympics?

CRICKET
RECORD BREAKERS

1

Which batsman was the first to score 100 first-class hundreds?

2

Who holds the record for most Test appearances?

3

Who made the highest individual Test score for Pakistan?

4

Which bowler had the biggest wicket haul in a Text series?

5

What is the best return in a Test innings by an Indian bowler?

6

Which country has won the cricket World Cup most times?

7

Who has scored the only individual century in a Twenty20 international?

8

Which Test match lasted longest?

9

Who was the second player to hit 6 sixes on an over?

10

Who holds the Test record for wicketkeeping dismissals?

11

What is the highest partnership for any wicket in Tests?

12

Who has the highest career Test batting average?

....

1

"Whispering Death"

....

2

"The Turbanator"

....

3

"The Cat"

....

4

"Tugger"

....

5

"The Croucher"

....

6

"Zulu"

....

7

"The Old Man"

....

8

"Big Bird"

....

9

"Lord Ted"

....

10

"The Little Master"

....

11

"Fiery"

....

12

"Nugget"

....

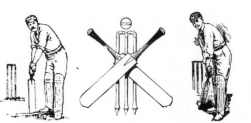

CRICKET
ALL-ROUNDERS

1

Which great England batsman played for Arsenal?

2

Who played cricket for Australia and England, and rugby for England?

3

For which Football League team did Ian Botham play?

4

Which England cricketer was offered the throne of Albania?

5

Which England captain became an eminent psychoanalyst?

6

Which England captain won an Olympic boxing gold in 1908?

7

Who was the last Englishman to play both international cricket and football?

8

Who is the only Nobel Prizewinner to appear in *Wisden's Alamanac*?

9

Which Pakistan all-rounder founded a new political party in 1996?

10

Which England cricketer appeared in *The Prisoner of Zenda*?

11

Which great Australian all-rounder was a fighter pilot in World War Two?

12

Which West Indian cricketer was given a Life Peerage in 1969?

CRICKET
INITIALS: WHAT ARE THE FULL NAMES OF...?

1

E. deC. W.

2

R.G.D.W.

3

D.I.G.

4

G. St A. S.

5

B.L. d'O.

6

D.K.L.

7

M.C.C.

8

G.D.McG.

9

I.T.B.

10

K.P.P.

11

D.G.B.

12

W.J.O'R.

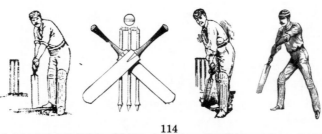

CRICKET
ANCIENT HISTORY

1

Why are the stumps so called?

2

What was the nickname of 18th-century cricket legend
William Beldham?

3

When is the first record of overarm bowling – 1762, 1812 or 1862?

4

For which county did W G Grace play from 1868?

5

What was special about the first Australian team to tour England
in 1868?

6

Why is the wicket so called?

7

What was the destination of England's first touring team in 1859?

8

Which Australian faced the first ever ball in Test cricket in 1876?

9

What type of ball was invented by B J T Bosanquet in the early 1900s?

10

Who topped both batting and bowling averages in the 1905 Ashes series?

11

Which country did K S Ranjitsinhji play for from 1896?

12

Which Australian scored a classic pre-lunch 100 at Manchester in 1902?

1

What was the first English one-day knock-out competition?

2

Which pair invented a way of calculating targets in rain-affected games?

3

Which countries will host the 2011 World Cup?

4

The Ford Ranger Cup is played for in which country?

5

Which country currently has a 100% record in ODIs?

6

What is the biggest total yet made in a one-day international?

7

Who has the best bowling figures in a one-day international?

8

What feat by Brett Lee in 2007 was a Twenty20 first?

9

Which player has hit most 6s in Twenty20 internationals?

10

Which country has recorded most consecutive ODI victories?

11

Which team won the ICC Women's World Cup in 2008/9?

12

What is the highest individual score ever made in the Women's World Cup?

CRICKET
CRICKET QUOTES: WHO SAID...?

....

1

"We'll get 'em in singles, Wilfred."

....

2

"Let's give it a bit of humpty."

....

3

"Sorry, Doc, she slipped."

....

4

"What do they know of cricket, who only cricket know?"

....

5

"The bowler's Holding, the batsman's Willey."

....

6

"First thing, we'll have no more bloody swearing!"

....

7

"Cricket civilizes people. I want everyone to play cricket in Zimbabwe."

....

8

"One-day cricket is like fast food: no-one wants to cook."

....

9

"I was never coached; I was never told how to hold a bat."

....

10

"No good hitting me there, mate, there's nothing to damage."

....

11

"I'll make them grovel."

....

12

"Yes! No! Wait!."

....

CRICKET
IN THE FAMILY

1

Which England player's father and grandfather played for West Indies?

2

What relation were Pakistan's Hanif, Sadiq and Wazir Mohammed?

3

What are the first names of Shaun Pollock's Test-playing father and uncle?

4

Which of two Australian brothers was known as "Afghanistan"?

5

Whose father captained New Zealand between 1945 and 1951?

6

Which of W.G. Grace's brothers played only one Test?

7

Which three sets of brothers played for Surrey in 1999?

8

What relation was Hansie Cronje to Jonathan Agnew?

9

Which Yorkshire-born sportsman has Viv Richards as godfather?

10

Which pair of brothers – and their grandfather – captained Australia?

11

Which cousins of Imran Khan also captained Pakistan?

12

Which English county cricketer's grandfather was once Doctor Who?

1

Which way does an outswinger move?

2

What is a beamer?

3

What's the term for getting two golden ducks in the same match?

4

Which way does a doosra move?

5

What is the splice of a bat?

6

What kind of ball is a creeper?

7

Which side of the wicket does gully stand?

8

What is a Chinaman?

9

Where is the return crease?

10

When a new batsman asks for "two", what is required?

11

What kind of ball is a googly?

12

What is a "coffin" used for?

1

Where is the Queen's Park Oval?

2

Which English county side has its HQ at Trent Bridge?

3

Why is Lord's Cricket Ground so called?

4

Which Australian ground is known as "The Wacker"?

5

Where is the Wanderers' Stadium?

6

Where did Sri Lanka play their first ever Test Match in 1982?

7

Which is Durham's home ground?

8

Which island has the newest Test venue in the West Indies?

9

Which is the largest cricket stadium in the world?

10

In which city is the Wankhede Stadium?

11

Which is the main Test ground on New Zealand's South Island?

12

Which Pakistani Test ground is on the edge of the Sind Desert?

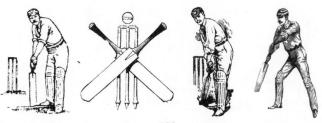

1

Whose 75-minute hundred brought an Ashes victory at the Oval in 1902?

2

When did Brian Lara first make the highest-ever individual Test score?

3

Who is the only Test batsman to score over 300 in a single day?

4

What was Derek Randall's score in the second innings of the Centenary Test?

5

Whose 281 at Calcutta in 2001 brought a sensational victory over Australia?

6

Which Australian scored a brilliant 187 in the first "Bodyline" Test?

7

How many 100s did Ian Botham score in the 1981 Ashes series?

8

Who has scored the most first-class centuries?

9

What was special about Nathan Astle's 222 against England in 2001?

10

Who made the most consecutive Test 100s?

11

Who made the most runs in a single session in Test cricket?

12

Against which county did Gary Sobers hit 6 sixes in an over?

1

How many runs did Jim Laker concede while taking
19 Australian wickets?

2

Who took 6 English wickets in 23 balls at Lord's in 1878?

3

What is the best bowling return by an Australian in a Test innings?

4

Who took over 200 Test wickets bowling left-arm swing and spin?

5

Who took 7 for 12 at Kingston, Jamaica, in 2004?

6

Who is the only bowler after Laker to take 10 wickets in a Test innings?

7

Who said "You guys are history", before taking 9 for 57?

8

In which year did Shane Warne bowl "the ball of the century"?

9

Who had 14 Test victims on a flat Oval wicket in 1976?

10

Who has taken the most first-class wickets?

11

Who has taken most Test wickets?

12

How many wickets did Bob Massie take at Lord's in 1972?

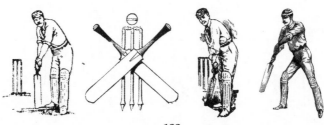

CRICKET
LONG TERM, SHORT TERM

1

Who had the longest-ever Test career?

2

Who was the youngest-ever Test cricketer?

3

Who has played the most consecutive Test matches?

4

Which is the longest first-class innings?

5

What was unique about the Test career of J C W MacBryan?

6

What is the lowest first class total made this century?

7

What weird fate befell A J Harris at Nottingham in 2003?

8

Which is the shortest complete innings (by balls bowled)?

9

What is the slowest run-rate by a side in a complete Test innings?

10

Which country has suffered the most consecutive ODI defeats?

11

Who has bowled the most balls in an ODI career?

12

Which famously slow-scoring batsman was nicknamed "Barnacle"?

CRICKET
ASHES SPECIAL

1

What was burned to create "The Ashes"?

2

What trophy is now presented to the winning Ashes captain?

3

Which Ashes captain said, "I've not travelled 6,000 miles to make friends"?

4

Who bowled Bradman for a duck in his last Ashes innings?

5

Who captained the 1981 Australian tourists?

6

What was England's winning margin in the 4th Test of 1982/83?

7

How many times has an Ashes series been won 5-0?

8

How many Ashes Tests have there been (to 2007)?

9

Which side has won most?

10

Who has made the most 100s in Ashes games?

11

Who took the most wickets in an Ashes series?

12

Who faced the first ball in England/ Australia Tests?

CRICKET
WHICH SURNAMES?

1

Kim, Merv, Phillip

2

Geraint, Jeff, Dean

3

Collie, M J K., Graeme

4

Basil, Roland, Mark

5

Tom, Vic, Richie

6

Barry, Jack, Viv

7

Ian, Greg, Trevor

8

Mark, "Tonker", Bruce

9

Shane, Willie, Chester

10

Deryck, J T, Junior

11

John, F S, Archie

12

"Pasty", Chris, Lord George Robert Canning

CRICKET
IN THE FIELD

1

In which year did "Copley's catch" turn an Ashes Test?

2

Which fielder has held the most catches in Tests?

3

Which keeper holds the record for stumpings in a Test innings?

4

Which fielder has held the most catches in an ICC Twenty20 game?

5

Which West Indies captain of the 1970s was also a brilliant cover point?

6

Whose catch gave Fred Trueman his 300th Test victim in 1964?

7

Which keeper claimed the most first-class dismissals in a career?

8

Which fielder took the most catches in a first-class match?

9

Whom did Andrew Strauss catch miraculously at Trent Bridge in 2005?

10

"Caught who?, bowled Lillee" is the most frequent Test dismissal?

11

Which country lost the most batsmen to runouts in a single Test?

12

Who has taken the most catches in an ODI career?

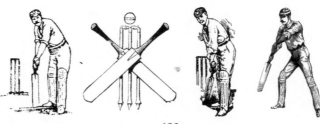

CRICKET
WORLD CUP

1

Which country won the first World Cup in 1975?

2

Which country hosted the 2003 World Cup?

3

Which left-hander famously hit Lillee for 35 runs in 10 balls in 1975?

4

What is the biggest margin of victory in a World Cup game?

5

Which side has won the most World Cup matches?

6

Who holds the record for the highest individual score?

7

Who has the best career bowling average in World Cup games?

8

In which year did India win the World Cup?

9

What is the highest ever batting partnership?

10

Which team has been World Cup runner-up most often?

11

Who has played most World Cup matches as captain?

12

Who has the highest World Cup batting average?

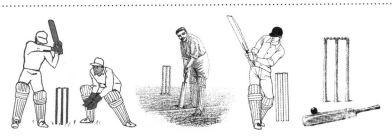

1
501

2
111

3
19

4
1877

5
365

6
8 for 43

7
87

8
1954

9
61,760

10
0.06 of a run

11
56 balls

12
666666

  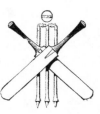 

1

When did the first women's Test match take place?

2

Who won it?

3

What is the highest team innings total in a women's Test?

4

In which year was the first Women's World Cup?

5

How many teams are taking part in the first women's
Twenty20 tournament?

6

On which famous ground did women play their first international
in 1976?

7

Who holds the record for highest individual Test innings?

8

Who has captained a Test side most often?

9

Who has taken the most wickets in a Test career?

10

What is the lowest team total in a One Day Innings?

11

What is the best Test Match bowling analysis?

12

Which team has won the most Test Matches?

1

Which county were the very first official English champions in 1890?

2

What was the Friends Provident Trophy originally known as?

3

Which Arab country takes part in the Asia Cup?

4

Which trophy is competed for by Australia and New Zealand?

5

What is Australia's Sheffield Shield competition now known as?

6

In which year did cricket feature in an Olympic Games?

7

How many first class teams take part in West Indies domestic competitions?

8

Who were champions of the first Indian Premier League in 2008?

9

In which country was the second IPL season held?

10

In which country do teams compete for the Quaid-e-Azam Trophy?

11

Which English county has won the Championship most times?

12

In which year was the County Championship split into two divisions?

1

Which two golfers have won three major championships in one year?

2

Which golfer has won the most majors?

3

Which Englishman has won the most majors?

4

How many majors have been won by a Frenchman?

5

Which two players have won golf's Triple Crown?

6

Who is the oldest PGA Tour winner?

7

Who was the first golfer to shoot 59 in a PGA Tour event?

8

What is the record high score for a hole in a major?

9

Who is the youngest player to win the Masters?

10

Who was the first golfer to wear plus fours?

11

Who won the British Open belt outright in 1870 after three successive victories?

12

Which Fijian has most PGA Tour victories?

126

....

1

"The Big Easy"

....

2

"The Black Knight"

....

3

"El Niño"

....

4

"Golden Bear"

....

5

"The Wee Ice Mon"

....

6

"The King"

....

7

"The Haig"

....

8

"The Merry Mex"

....

9

"The Squire"

....

10

"Wild Thing"

....

11

"The Pink Panther"

....

12

"Chocolate Soldier"

....

1

When would a player use a fairway wood?

2

What was a jigger?

3

What is the name for a club head with a depression on the back?

4

What is balata used for?

5

What part of a club is the hosel?

6

What is the slang for matchplay in which each hole is worth points or money?

7

When is a ball stone dead?

8

What is a mulligan?

9

What is the Vardon grip?

10

What is a sclaff?

11

What is "dance floor" a slang name for?

12

What happens when a ball plugs?

GOLF
ANCIENT HISTORY

1

What did medieval golfers putt into?

2

What distinction is claimed by Musselburgh Old Links?

3

Which English king played golf while held captive by the Scots in 1646?

4

In which country was the first 18-hole course laid out?

5

What substance was used for making golf balls from 1848?

6

In which year was the rubber-cored ball invented?

7

Who won the very first Open Championship in Scotland in 1861?

8

Which scoring term, based on a popular song, was first used in 1890?

9

In which year did Harry Vardon win his first British Open?

10

Which major British course was opened in 1901?

11

Who was the first native-born American to win the US Open?

12

Why did the air-filled golf ball, introduced in 1906, fail to catch on?

GOLF
COURSES OF THE WORLD

1
What famous course is known as the "Home of Golf"?

2
What is unique about the Coober Pedy course in Australia?

3
In which Asian country is the Blue Canyon course?

4
Which is the major golf course on Mallorca?

5
Which US golf course was designed by Bobby Jones and
Alister McKenzie?

6
Which course has hosted more major competitions than any other
in the US?

7
Which great European course was originally known as Los Aves?

8
Which king became patron of the Royal and Ancient in 1834?

9
Which course is home to the world's oldest golf club?

10
Which US course was founded by George Crump?

11
Which Australian Sandbelt course was opened in 1931?

12
Which course is known as "Scotland's Pebble Beach"?

1

"It is the best game in the world at which to be bad."

2

"Golf, like the measles, should be caught young."

3

"If you drink, don't drive. Don't even putt."

4

"Golf is a good walk spoiled."

5

"Golf is a sport for white men dressed like black pimps."

6

"The harder you work, the luckier you get."

7

"Golf is deceptively simple and endlessly complicated."

8

"If you want to increase your success rate, double your failure rate."

9

"I like trying to win. That's what golf is all about."

10

"My swing is so bad I look like a caveman killing his lunch."

11

"I'll shoot my age if I have to live to be 105."

12

"The most important shot in golf is the next one."

NAME THE YEAR (1)

1

In which year did Arnold Palmer first win the US Open?

2

In which year was there no PGA Championship?

3

When was the Royal and Ancient Golf Club originally founded?

4

In which year was the American PGA formed?

5

When did Great Britain first win the Ryder Cup?

6

In which year did Zach Johnson win the Masters?

7

When did Tony Jacklin win the British Open?

8

In which year did Tiger Woods win his first Major?

9

In which year did Padraig Harrington win the PGA Championship?

10

When was the very first Masters?

11

When did Gary Player become the first non-American to win the Masters?

12

In which year was the British Open staged in Northern Ireland?

1

In which calendar month does the Open take place?

2

What is unique among the Majors in the Open's rules for tied players?

3

What was the original trophy of the Open?

4

Who was the last amateur to win the Open?

5

Who was the only Irish Open winner before Padraig Harrington?

6

Who holds the record for most rounds under par?

7

In which year did the Open become an official part of the PGA Tour?

8

At which club was the first ever Open played?

9

Who has gained the most Open victories?

10

Who is the youngest winner of the Open?

11

Who is the oldest?

12

Where will the 2011 Open be played?

GOLF
THE US OPEN

1

What happens if the US Open is tied after four rounds?

2

How many times has the Open gone to a "sudden-death" playoff?

3

Where was the first US Open played in 1895?

4

Who won it?

5

Who was the last European player to win the Open?

6

Which players are exempt from qualifying?

7

Who was champion in 2007?

8

What was special about Hale Irwin's victory in 1990?

9

Who holds the record for most strokes under par after four rounds?

10

Where will the US Open be staged in 2011?

11

Who has won most consecutive championships?

12

Which four players share the record for most victories overall?

GOLF
THE MASTERS

1

How does the entry for the Masters differ from other Majors?

2

Who has won the most Masters tournaments?

3

In which calendar month is the Masters played?

4

How many holes-in-one were recorded at the 2002 tournament?

5

Which year was the first Masters?

6

Who has played in the most tournaments?

7

What was the significant achievement of Lee Elder in 1975?

8

How many black members did Augusta National have at the time?

9

Who won the 2008 Masters?

10

Who was the last English player to win?

11

Which two golfers share the course record of 63?

12

Who was the youngest player to win the Masters?

GOLF
THE PGA CHAMPIONSHIP

1

When was the US PGA Championship established?

2

Who was the first winner?

3

In which year was the format changed from match play to stroke play?

4

Who was PGA champion in 2008?

5

Who was the last Australian to win?

6

Who was the last of the match play champions?

7

And who was the first of the stroke play champions?

8

Who was the youngest ever winner?

9

Where will the Championship be held in 2011?

10

What is the lowest score for 72 holes?

11

Which pair share the record for greatest number of wins?

12

What is the name of the trophy awarded to the PGA champion?

1

In which year was the Women's British Open established?

2

Who won the event in 2008?

3

Which British queen is said to have first used the word "caddy"?

4

In what year was the first British Ladies' Golf Championship?

5

Who was the first winner?

6

Who was the first American to win the competition?

7

Which woman golfer has the most professional wins?

8

Which Major was won by Lorena Ochoa in 2008?

9

Who is the only woman to have won five different Majors?

10

Which teams compete for the Solheim Cup?

11

Who was chosen as Female Athlete of the Year in 1978 and 1985?

12

Who was the first woman to win a medal at a men's US Open qualifier?

1

In which year was the first Ryder Cup competition?

2

Which is the only tournament since 1945 to have been postponed?

3

Who was Europe's winning captain in 2004?

4

How long does a Ryder Cup tournament last?

5

What was the profession of Samuel Ryder?

6

In which year was the first tied Ryder Cup?

7

After which Cup did some of the US team apologize for their behaviour?

8

When was the Ryder Cup last played in England?

9

How many times have Europe won the tournament?

10

Which player has appeared most times in a team?

11

Which two players scored holes-in-one in 2006?

12

Who is the youngest Ryder Cup player?

1

Which two sides compete in the President's Cup?

2

What is the amateur version of the Ryder Cup for men?

3

What is the US v Britain competition for women amateurs?

4

Which sides take part in the Dynasty Cup?

5

What is the age limit in the Tommy Bahama Challenge?

6

What is the tournament played between Asia and Europe?

7

Which European event was founded by Severiano Ballesteros?

8

Who compete in the Palmer Cup?

9

What is the age limit for the Junior Ryder Cup?

10

Which women's event pits Asians against the rest of the world?

11

In which year was the Hong Kong Open established?

12

What replaced the Order of Merit in 2009?

1

Who was the first sportsman to be given a Broadway tickertape parade?

2

Who recovered from a major car crash in 1953 to win three Majors?

3

Who won the European Order of Merit seven times, but never a Major?

4

Which Spaniard became the youngest Open winner in the last century?

5

Which woman won the 1986 British Open and the 1987 US Open?

6

Which women's golfer won athletics golds at the 1932 Olympics?

7

Who is the oldest winner on the PGA Tour?

8

Which five-time Open winner helped found the British PGA?

9

What were Arnold Palmer's devoted fans known as?

10

Who always wears a red shirt during a Major's final round?

11

Who was the first woman to compete in a men's PGA event?

12

Why is Greg Norman known as the "Great White Shark"?

1

What is the largest winning margin in a Major?

2

Who made most money in a year on the PGA Tour?

3

Who has made the lowest 18-hole score on the LPGA Tour?

4

Who has finished in the top 5 most often in the US Masters?

5

Apart from Americans, which nationality has won the most Majors?

6

Which two players have made the cut in most consecutive Masters?

7

Who holds the record for most birdies in a single Masters round?

8

Who recorded the lowest 72-hole score in the British Open?

9

What's unique about Old Tom Morris's 13-stroke victory at the 1862 Open?

10

Which quartet share the record for lowest score in a US Open round?

11

Which venue has hosted most US Opens?

12

Who is the oldest winner of the PGA Championship?

1

In which year was the European PGA formed?

2

Which was the first European Tour event held outside Europe?

3

In which year was the first Dubai Desert Classic?

4

Which East Asian city was first included in the Tour in 1992?

5

Who was winner of the last Order of Merit in 2008?

6

Who finished top of the Order of Merit most often?

7

Who was Rookie of the Year in 2000?

8

And who was Player of the Year in 2000?

9

Who has won the Player of the Year award most times?

10

Who has most wins on the European Tour?

11

When was the Ladies' European Tour founded?

12

Who was the women's Order of Merit winner in 2008?

1

The HQ of the PGA Tour is in which US state?

2

In which year was the title "PGA Tour" officially adopted?

3

Which is the only European country visited by the Tour?

4

Which is the first tournament of the Tour season?

5

Which PGA Tour competition was founded by Jack Nicklaus?

6

Who was the Tour's top money-earner in 2008?

7

But who recorded the most wins?

8

In which country is the HSBC Champions competition played?

9

Who had the most wins in the very first US (pre-PGA) Tour?

10

In which year was that?

11

Which two players have topped the money list most times?

12

Who was Tour Rookie of the Year in 2008?

1

When did Europe first contest the Ryder Cup?

2

In which year was the World Matchplay Championship founded?

3

When did "Wild Thing" John Daly win the PGA Championship?

4

In which years did Nick Faldo have back-to-back Masters wins?

5

When did the first Scotsman win the US Open?

6

In which year did Australian Geoff Ogilvy win the US Open?

7

When did the first non-Scot win the British Open?

8

In which year was Tiger Woods born?

9

Which year's Ryder Cup was known as "The War on the Shore"?

10

Which year was the last Masters decided by a sudden death play-off?

11

In which year was golf last included as an Olympic sport?

12

In which year did Jack Nicklaus win his last major?

GOLF
NICKNAMES – WHO WAS KNOWN AS...? (2)

1

"Babe"

2

"The Big Wiesy"

3

"Double D"

4

"El Gato"

5

"Champagne Tony"

6

"The Walrus"

7

"Zinger"

8

"Slammin' Sam"

9

"Ohio Fats"

10

"Lefty"

11

"The Hawk"

12

"Huckleberry Dillinger"

1

Which country has never got beyond the first round in
9 World Cup finals?

2

Which two players played for Italy in both the 1934 and 1938 finals?

3

Which Peruvian player scored a hat-trick against Iran in the 1978 finals?

4

Which city staged the opening match of the 1994 finals?

5

Which two countries reached the last four at their first finals?

6

Which African nation played in their first World Cup finals in 1970?

7

Against whom did France gain their solitary point in 1966?

8

Who was Holland's first-choice keeper in the 1994 finals?

9

Who coached the victorious Uruguayan team in 1930?

10

How many times has Romania qualified for the finals?

11

Who scored twice for Chile at the 1998 finals?

12

Who did England meet in their opening match in the 2002 finals?

1

"The Galloping Major"

2

"The Kaiser"

3

"King Eric"

4

"Giraffe"

5

"Piranha"

6

"Little Bird"

7

"The Black Tulip"

8

"The Flea"

9

"Psycho"

10

"Ragazzo d'Oro"

11

"The White Pele"

12

"Dr Jekyll"

1

Who was voted Oceania's Player of the 20th-Century?

2

In which country do Universitatea and Otelul Galati play?

3

Who won the Bundesliga for the third successive year in 2000/1?

4

In which Italian city do Atalanta play?

5

Which Italian club are known as the "Nerazzurri"?

6

Who was Spain's national coach from 1982 to 1988?

7

Which Uruguayan team won the first World Club Championship?

8

Which club has won most Swedish league titles?

9

Who were the first Argentinian club to win the Copa Libertadores?

10

How many times have Olympique Lyonnais won the French League?

11

On which island are Cagliari based?

12

Of which African nation was Didier Notheaux appointed coach in 1998?

1

In which city do Fiorentina play?

2

Which ground was built in Rio de Janeiro for the 1950 World Cup?

3

The Bosuil Stadium is the home of which Belgian club?

4

Which Danish club play at the Parken?

5

Which German club play at the Volksparkstadion?

6

Which is the biggest stadium in Europe?

7

At which ground do Juventus play?

8

Which ground has the biggest capacity in the world?

9

Which club plays at the Bernabeu?

10

Which club plays at the Phillips Stadium?

11

In which Italian city is the home ground of Sampdoria?

12

In which country do Cruz Azul and Atletico Morelia play?

1

Which two goalkeepers have captained Italy to victory in the World Cup?

2

Whose goal for Italy put Ireland out of the 1990 World Cup?

3

Who was Argentina's goalkeeper in the 1990 World Cup Final?

4

Who scored 316 goals in 294 games for Benfica?

5

For which country did Bernard Lama play international football?

6

What nationality was keeper Hans Segers?

7

Whose Real Madrid goalscoring record did Raul overhaul in 2009?

8

Who holds the international goalscoring record for Caribbean countries?

9

For which club did Lev Yashin make 326 appearances?

2

Which keeper saved three penalties in the 2001 Champions' League Final?

11

Who has scored the most international goals for the USA?

12

Which Italian legend was given a free transfer by Juventus?

1

In which year did Colombia first qualify for the World Cup finals?

2

Who scored two penalties for England against Cameroon in 1990?

3

Who beat Tonga 22-0 and American Samoa 31-0 within two days in 2001?

4

Who was Scotland's leading goalscorer at the 1974 finals?

5

Who were England's first opponents in the 1970 finals?

6

On which racecourse did England train before the 1950 finals?

7

Who did West Germany beat 5-0 in their first match in 1966?

8

Who were the only country to win all three group matches in 1978?

9

Which two players have won the World Cup as both player and coach?

10

Who is the overall leading goalscorer in World Cup finals?

11

Which two players have appeared in most tournaments?

12

Which World Cup scoring record is held by France's Just Fontaine?

1

"The Dons" (in England?)

2

"The Dons" (in Scotland?)

3

"The Baggies"

4

"The Hornets"

5

"The Jags"

6

"The Binos"

7

"The Wee Rovers"

8

"The Elephants"

9

"Los Cules"

10

"I Viola"

11

"Die Roten"

12

"O Glorioso"

1

Which team played in every French Cup final from 1946 to 1955?

2

Which club won the Spanish League and Cup double in 1975?

3

Which European country beat Zambia 9-0 in 1994?

4

For which country did Toni Polster win a record number of caps?

5

In which country are the clubs Birkirkara and Sliema?

6

Who won the Italian League in 1997?

7

Which Norwegian played for a Spanish team in the 2001
UEFA Cup Final?

8

Which country's cup was won by Etzella Ettlebruck in 2001?

9

Who were Italian League Champions for the only time in 1970?

10

Viborg won which country's Cup competition in 2000?

11

Which Spanish star was kidnapped in Venezuela in 1963?

12

Which Dutch international was banned by FIFA for failing a drugs
test in 2001?

1

When was Pele appointed Brazil's Minister for Sport?

2

Which is Spain's oldest club?

3

What nationality is Gabriel Batistuta?

4

Which Bulgarian club plays at the Bulgarska Armia Stadium?

5

When did Johann Cruyff make his international debut?

6

Which amateur team reached the 2001 German Cup Final?

7

In which country do a team called "The Strongest" play?

8

In what colour shirts do Australia play?

9

Who was the first Brazilian to play for Real Madrid?

10

With which German club did Uwe Seeler play his entire career?

11

Which Maldini was Italian national coach?

12

Who won their 13th Russian League title in 1999?

1

Who defeated Liverpool in the 2005 final of the Club World championship?

2

In which year was the very first Copa America?

3

Which country won it?

4

Which country won the Copa America in 2004 and 2007?

5

For which country does Lionel Messi play?

6

What is the name of Latin America's top club tournament?

7

Who was Brazil's coach at the 1982 World Cup?

8

In which country do the clubs Monagas and Carabobo play?

9

Which Argentine defender scored 20 goals in 65 internationals?

10

In what colour shirts do Peru play?

11

Which Brazilian exponent of the "banana shot" scored 26 goals in 94 games?

12

In which year did Diego Maradona win his first cap?

1

In which year was the European Cup originally founded?

2

When did it officially become the Champions' League?

3

How much did the 2009 champions receive for winning?

4

Which team beat Eintracht 7-3 to win the 1960 final?

5

Which team had Manchester United played just before their 1958 aircrash tragedy?

6

What was the half-time score in the 2005 final in Istanbul?

7

Which French club was stripped of the crown in 1993?

8

Which was the first club to lose a cup tie on away goals (in 1967/8)?

9

Who won the 2001 Champions' League?

10

Which was the first Turkish club to win a European title?

11

Who were the first Greek club to reach a European Cup final?

12

Whose penalty won the 1985 Cup for Juventus?

1

What was the first women's football tournament in Britain?

2

In which year did the FA ban women's football?

3

When was the UEFA Cup for women launched?

4

Which country hosted the first Women World Cup in 1991?

5

Which team won the 1999 World Cup?

6

In which country did a female team swap shorts for miniskirts in 2008?

7

What is the main women's cup competition in Spain?

8

Which 2002 film features a football-loving Sikh girl?

9

Which continent is home to the CAF Women's Championship?

10

Which English team won the League and Cup double in 2006?

11

Who were silver medallists in the 2008 Olympic women's football?

12

Who was top scorer in the 2008 Olympics?

1

In which year were the first European Championship finals held?

2

Which was the host country?

3

Which nation has won the title most times?

4

How many times have England been champions or runners-up?

5

Who is the top goal scorer overall in European finals?

6

Who scored Sweden's winning goal against England in 1992?

7

Which nation finished third in the 1964 tournament?

8

Why did Greece refuse to play Albania in a 1962 qualifier?

9

How many years separate Spain's 2008 title from their first?

10

Who was top individual scorer at the 2008 tournament?

11

Against whom did San Marino score their first ever Championship goal?

12

Which two Arsenal players were in the 1996 Dutch squad?

1

Who were the first black African country to reach the World Cup finals?

2

Which two nations did Rudolf Vytlacil lead to the World Cup finals?

3

Which team played 15 qualifying games in the 1982 World Cup?

4

Which Belgian appeared in three successive finals?

5

Who played for Hungary in 1954 and Spain in 1962?

6

In 1990, which Italian keeper did not concede a goal for 517 minutes?

7

Which Argentinian eventually beat him?

8

Who scored twice in the 1958 final and once in the 1970 final?

9

What was Anatoly Puzach's claim to fame?

10

How many tournaments have been held in all?

11

How many different nations have won the World Cup?

12

Which team came fourth in the 2006 World Cup?

1

"Donkey"

2

"Golden Ponytail"

3

"Beast"

4

"Black Panther"

5

"Sparky"

6

"Super Pippo"

7

"Bald Eagle"

8

"The Wizard of Dribble"

9

"Fenomeno"

10

"Ready Teddy"

11

"Pitbull"

12

"Black Spider"

1

Which club won the Greek Cup in 2000?

2

Which African country beat Spain in their first game in the
1998 World Cup?

3

Which country's League did Bangu win for the first time in 1967?

4

Which Dynamo Kiev player was European Footballer of the Year in 1975?

5

For which French club did David Ginola make his League debut?

6

When was Roberto Baggio transferred for £7.7 million?

7

In which African country do Esperance play?

8

Which German club won the Bundesliga five times in the 1970s?

9

Which Bulgarian was named European Player of the Year in 1994?

10

What is unique about Udo Lattek's managerial career?

11

How many World Cup finals have China appeared in?

12

Which French writer played in goal for a cup-winning Algerian
football club?

1

What was Alexander Cartwright's main achievement as "father of baseball"?

2

Which pioneering professional team was founded in 1869?

3

What is the distance between the pitching rubber and the home plate?

4

What makes the Chicago Cubs so special?

5

What was Ty Cobb's record career batting average?

6

And what was his nickname?

7

In which year was the modern World Series established?

8

How many players were indicted in the Black Sox Scandal of 1919?

9

Which great pitcher was known as "Big Train"?

10

Which team has won the most World Series titles?

11

What rule change was forced by the tragic death of Ray Chapman in 1920?

12

What was the full name of "Babe" Ruth?

1

What was the unusual distinction of Eddie Gaedel?

2

Whose record did Babe Ruth beat with his 60th home run in 1927?

3

In which year was the Baseball Hall of Fame opened?

4

In how many consecutive games did Joe DiMaggio hit successfully in 1941?

5

Who was the first African-American officially to play major league?

6

In which year was he signed?

7

Which pitcher won a record 31 games in 1968?

8

Who said [of astroturf] "If a horse can't eat it, I don't want to play on it"?

9

Who was known as "Luscious Luke"?

10

In which year did the Tampa Bay Devil Rays join the American League?

11

When was the World Series cancelled for only the second time?

12

Who broke Lou Gehrig's consecutive game record in 1995?

1

Who said "no boy from a rich family ever made the big leagues"?

2

Who was known as "Knucksie"?

3

Which team won the 1938 baseball World Cup?

4

Which player hit the most home runs in a career?

5

Who holds the record for most strikeouts in a season?

6

Who stole most bases in a career?

7

Whose nickname was "Cool Papa"?

8

What is a "can of corn"?

9

Who called himself "the luckiest man on the face of this Earth"?

10

Whose nickname was "Stan the Man"?

11

Whose name is on the annual awards for outstanding hitters in each league?

12

Which New York Yankee had a cartoon character named after him?

OTHER TEAM SPORTS
HOCKEY (1)

1

From which French word does the name "hockey" originate?

2

Who took part in the first hockey international in 1895?

3

When was hockey first played in the Olympics?

4

Which team has won hockey gold in the Olympics eight times?

5

Which hockey-like game developed in Scotland in the Middle Ages?

6

How far apart are hockey goal posts?

7

Who won the Women's World Cup in 2006?

8

Which city hosted the first Champion's Trophy in 1978?

9

Who is Great Britain's record goal scorer in men's hockey?

10

What Olympic first was achieved by Nova Perris-Kneebone in 1996?

11

Which state cricketer also played 234 hockey matches for Australia?

12

When was synthetic grass first used for hockey in the Olympics?

1

Which country hosted the 2006 World Cup?

2

Which country has won the World Cup most times?

3

What is England's best performance in the World Cup?

4

What was Argentina's winning score in the 2008 Women's Champion's Trophy?

5

Which two sides have been Men's Champions nine times?

6

Which country won the 2009 Men's Asia Cup?

7

Which hockey player recited the Oath at the opening of the 2000 Olympics?

8

Who is England's most-capped men's international?

9

How long is a standard hockey pitch?

10

Which legendary Indian forward scored 38 goals in Olympic matches?

11

How many times do players tap sticks at a bully-off?

12

What is a "wall pass"?

1

Of which country is ice hockey the official winter sport?

2

In which year was ice hockey first played in the Olympics?

3

Which country won gold at the 1936 Olympics?

4

From which Gaelic term is the word "puck" derived?

5

In which city was the first organized ice hockey game?

6

In which year was the World Hockey Association formed?

7

What position is taken by a "blueliner"?

8

Whose nickname was "Old Hardrock"?

9

When was the first ice hockey World Championship?

10

Which US team is known as "The Blueshirts"?

11

How wide is the goal cage?

12

Who won ice hockey gold at the 2006 Winter Olympics?

1

How long is a period in an ice hockey game?

2

Who was known as "Sid the Kid"?

3

Which Canadian team has the nickname "The Flying Frenchmen"?

4

In which year did Wayne Gretzky retire?

5

What kind of offence is a "butt-ending"?

6

What three elements make up a "Gordie Howe hat-trick"?

7

What nationality was Jaromir Jagr?

8

What is Wayne Gretzky's league goal record?

9

Whose nickname was "The Pocket Rocket"?

10

What kind of move is a "deke"?

11

Who is Britain's top points scorer in internationals?

12

Which is the oldest professional trophy in North America?

OTHER TEAM SPORTS
AMERICAN FOOTBALL (1)

1

How long is an American football pitch?

2

In which year was the first Super Bowl?

3

Which annual contest was first played in 1875?

4

Whose changes to the line of scrimmage revolutionized the game in 1880?

5

How many fatalities were there during the infamous 1905 season?

6

Which great player devised the Notre Dame Box offense?

7

Who won the first Most Valuable Player award?

8

Whose nickname was "The Galloping Ghost"?

9

What are known as "the trenches"?

10

What is the trophy lifted by the winners of the Super Bowl?

11

Which great player appeared for the New York Jets from 1965 to 1988?

12

Who was known as "The Refrigerator"?

1

What is a "hail Mary"?

2

How many different bowl games were there in 2008?

3

What was the distinctive achievement of William "Pudge" Heffelfinger?

4

Whose nickname was "Crazy Legs"?

5

Who was first president of the American Professional FA?

6

In which year was the National Football League formed?

7

Which was the first NFL game to go into sudden death overtime?

8

Who scored most touchdowns in an NFL career?

9

Who was known as "Sweetness"?

10

Who played most seasons in the NFL?

11

Who holds the record for most pass attempts in one NFL game?

12

Which team have won the most Super Bowls?

1

Which US President went to college on a football scholarship?

2

Who was known as "The Flying Dutchman"?

3

In a game, who are known as the "zebras"?

4

In which city will the 2011 Super Bowl be staged?

5

After which player is the Green Bay Packers' stadium named?

6

Who was the first running back to gain over 2,000 yards in a season?

7

Which professional halfback won two Olympic golds in athletics?

8

In which country was points record holder Morton Andersen born?

9

Whose nickname was "Papa Bear"?

10

Who were the first winners of the World Bowl in 1991?

11

In which year was the AFL amalgamated with the NFL?

12

Who were runners-up in the 2009 NFL Championships?

1

What shape is an Australian Rules pitch?

2

Why was the game originally developed (according to legend)?

3

In which year was the first Premiership Trophy held?

4

Who are the only AFL team to have won four back-to-back Trophies?

5

How far can a player run with the ball before bouncing it?

6

In which month does the football season begin?

7

Which was the first South Australian team to join the AFL?

8

Who holds the career goalkicking record in the AFL?

9

Who has played the most League games?

10

Who has scored the most goals in a single game?

11

Who is the youngest player to make his AFL debut?

12

What is the highest team score in a League game?

OTHER TEAM SPORTS
GAELIC FOOTBALL AND HURLING

1

Which two teams play in the International Rules Series?

2

In which year were the All-Ireland Championships first held?

3

How does a player "solo" the ball?

4

Which great player led and later managed Dublin to All-Ireland victories?

5

Which has been the venue for almost every All-Ireland final?

6

Which team has won the All-Ireland finals most times?

7

How many people are there in a hurling team?

8

What is the name of the women's form of hurling?

9

Which hurling team has won the All-Ireland Championship most times?

10

In hurling, what is the *sliotar*?

11

Who is the only hurling player to have averaged over 10 points a game in a season?

12

Which Irish prime minister won medals in hurling and Gaelic football?

OTHER TEAM SPORTS
BASKETBALL (1)

1

In which year was basketball invented?

2

What was the forerunner of the hoop, used until 1906?

3

What kind of ball was originally used?

4

In which year was the Basketball Association of America formed?

5

What nationality is Chicago Bulls star Luol Deng?

6

Which country hosted the FIBA Championships in 2006?

7

What is the regulation length of an international basketball court?

8

Whose nickname was "The Big Diesel"?

9

What is meant by "hack-a shaq"?

10

Which team won the first ever NBA Championship in 1947?

11

In which year did basketball first feature at the Olympics?

12

Who are the two tallest players to have appeared in NBA games?

OTHER TEAM SPORTS
BASKETBALL (2)

1
What nationality is San Antonio Spurs' Tony Parker?

2
Who was known as "The Iceman"?

3
In which year did Michael Jordan make his League debut?

4
Which NBA player scored most points in a game?

5
Who has made most free throws in a game without a miss?

6
What is Kareem Abdul-Jabbar's record career points tally?

7
Which opposing teams scored the biggest combined points total
in a game?

8
Who has been the league's leading points scorer in a season most times?

9
What is the longest winning streak in the NBA?

10
Who was the first person to win the Most Valuable Player
award in 1956?

11
Whose nickname was "Chocolate Thunder"?

12
Which two players hold the record for most steals in a game?

1

Who is the first indigenous Australian to play in the NBA?

2

Who has played most games in an NBA season?

3

Who has played most minutes in an NBA finals game?

4

Who was known as "Doctor Dunkenstein"?

5

What are the most points scored in a game by a rookie?

6

Who is the oldest player to have scored 50 or more points in a game?

7

Who has scored most points in an NBA finals career?

8

Which team has won the NBA championship most times?

9

How many times did Magic Johnson retire?

10

Whose nickname was "The Worm"?

11

Which team were British Basketball League Champions in 2008?

12

Who has made most blocks in an NBA finals game?

OTHER TEAM SPORTS
LACROSSE

1

Which Native American people are reputed to have invented lacrosse?

2

Who won the Women's World Cup in 2005?

3

How many players are there in a men's lacrosse team?

4

In which country is lacrosse the official National Summer Sport?

5

What is box lacrosse?

6

Which English city will host the 2010 World Lacrosse Championships?

7

Which team other than the USA or Canada has played
a Championship final?

8

In which year was lacrosse last an official Olympic sport?

9

Who took first place at the 2008 European Lacrosse Championships?

10

Are men or women allowed to body-check in lacrosse?

11

What is the standard of a women's lacrosse game?

12

Which twin brothers share the record for goals in an NLL game?

OTHER TEAM SPORTS
MIXED BAG (1)

1

Which country hosted the 2007 Pétanque World Championships?

2

How does a boules team "do a Fanny"?

3

In boules, what is the "cochonnet"?

4

Which famous cricketer was first president of the English Bowling Association?

5

Which English bowls player won the world outdoor singles gold three times?

6

Which is the shot bowl?

7

Did Francis Drake win or lose his pre-Armada bowls game?

8

Which is the only year in which croquet was played at the Olympics?

9

What, in croquet, is the "carrot"?

10

Who became World Croquet singles champion in 2008?

11

What is the regulation uniform for pelota players?

12

What is the name of the wicker basket used to propel a pelota ball?

1

How long (to within five yards) is a regulation polo field?

2

How long does a polo "chukka" last?

3

Which country won the 2008 World Polo Championship?

4

Why was volleyball invented in 1895?

5

Which country won the women's Volleyball World Cup in 2007?

6

In which year was beach volleyball introduced to the Olympics?

7

How many players are there in a water polo team?

8

Which men's team won water polo gold at the 2008 Olympics?

9

What ball game was largely developed by Martina Bergman Osterberg?

10

Who won gold at the World Bandy Championships in 2009?

11

Which form of boules is pétanque derived from?

12

In bowls, what is the "kitty"?

1

In American football, what is "hang time"?

2

Which famous American footballer was played on film by
Ronald Reagan?

3

In Australian Rules, what is a "back pocket"?

4

How many substitutes per team are allowed in Australian Rules?

5

How high is a basketball hoop?

6

In baseball, who holds the all-time record for base hits?

7

What was the nickname of baseball player Willie Mays?

8

Where were basketball team the Lakers based before Los Angeles?

9

Which bowls player formed a classic partnership with David Bryant?

10

What, in bowls, is the "head"?

11

When was the All-Ireland Gaelic football final staged in New York?

12

Which country hosted the 2009 World Handball Championships?

1

How many substitutes are allowed in a game of field hockey?

2

How high does a hockey ball have to be hit at an opponent to be "dangerous"?

3

When did Great Britain win Olympic, world and European ice hockey titles?

4

Where, in ice hockey, is the "five-hole"?

5

How many steps can a netball player take before passing?

6

Why is jai alai (pelota) known as "the fastest ball game in the world"?

7

Which two world conquerors were known to be keen polo players?

8

In what gloomy setting was the game of rackets invented?

9

Which ball game features a "dedans", a "tambour" and a "hazard"?

10

In shinty, what is the "caman"?

11

What game was also known as "ladies' baseball", "kitten-ball" or "mush-ball"?

12

When was "Blood in the Water" water polo match between Hungary and USSR?

1

Who won the light-heavyweight gold at the 1960 Olympics?

2

Where did ancient Greek fighters wear their *himantes*?

3

Which heavyweight was known as "The Manassa Mauler"?

4

Who defeated John L. Sullivan in the first heavyweight title fight in 1892?

5

In which year were the Marquess of Queensberry Rules first drafted?

6

How long is the rest time between each round?

7

Which skilled defensive fighter was known as "The Mongoose"?

8

After whose death was the maximum number of rounds reduced to 12?

9

What does a boxer have to achieve to be a Triple Champion?

10

Who was the first Triple Champion?

11

Why was boxing dropped from the 1912 Stockholm Olympics?

12

Who won Olympic heavyweight gold on three consecutive occasions?

1

Which country has won most boxing medals at the Olympics?

2

How many women's boxing events were there at the 2008 Olympics?

3

Which two brothers held 4 versions of the heavyweight title between them?

4

Who gained the WBC lightweight title in April 2009?

5

In which year was the World Boxing Association founded?

6

Whose nickname was "The Real Deal"?

7

In boxing, what is a "palooka"?

8

Which great fighter was never knocked out in 202 bouts?

9

In which country did Muhammad Ali beat George Foreman in 1974?

10

Who was the first man to hold titles in 3 different divisions at the same time?

11

Which fighter was nicknamed "Hands of Stone"?

12

Who was the last undisputed heavyweight boxing champion?

OTHER INDIVIDUAL SPORTS
BOXING (3)

1

Which Briton was Olympic superweight champion in 2000?

2

What is the term for a foul blow to the back of the neck?

3

Which boxer was known as "Two-Ton Tony"?

4

Who was the first black heavyweight champion?

5

Who defeated Jack Dempsey in two classic fights in 1926 and 1927?

6

Which Olympic boxing champion captained England at cricket?

7

In which year did Lennox Lewis become WBC heavyweight champion?

8

What is the minimum weight for an Olympic super-heavyweight?

9

What nationality is Olympic welterweight champion
Bakhyt Sarsekbayev?

10

Which Welsh boxer retired undefeated in February 2009?

11

Whose nickname was "The Brown Bomber"?

12

In which year did Muhammad Ali defeat Sonny Liston for the
second time?

1

In which year was trampolining added to the Olympic programme?

2

Who won 3 consecutive women's golds at World Championships in the 90s?

3

How does a gymnast successfully "stick"?

4

How old was Nadia Comaneci when she got perfect scores at the 1976 Games?

5

Which year were women gymnasts allowed to compete in the Olympics?

6

Which much-loved gymnast was known as "The Sparrow from Minsk"?

7

What does the Greek word *gymnos* actually mean?

8

Which men's team won the 2007 Artistic Gymnastics World Championships?

9

Who won women's gold in the individual Artistic Gymnastics at the 2008 Games?

10

What, in gymnastics, is a "whip back"?

11

How many Olympic gold medals were won by Vitali Scherbo?

12

What is the standard height of a vaulting horse?

OTHER INDIVIDUAL SPORTS
TABLE TENNIS

1

When was competitive table tennis first introduced to the Olympics?

2

How long is a regulation table tennis table?

3

Who was the men's World Tennis Singles Champion in 2009?

4

Which city hosted the first World Championships in 1926?

5

What, in table tennis, is a "shakehands"?

6

Which great Hungarian player won 15 Championship titles in the 1930s?

7

Which European country won a table tennis medal at the 2008 Olympics?

8

Who won gold in the women's singles at Beijing in 2008?

9

Which Romanian player was unbeaten in singles from 1950 to 1955?

10

What are the "pips"?

11

What were early bats made of in Victorian England?

12

When did a US table tennis visit to China start a thaw in the Cold War?

1

What do two yellow dots on a squash ball signify?

2

Which great Australian player was unbeaten from 1962 to 1980?

3

Who has won the men's World Open Championship most times?

4

What type of shot is a "boast"?

5

What nationality was the legendary Abedel Fattah Amr?

6

Who is the first Asian woman to be ranked squash's World Number 1?

7

When was squash first included as an Olympic sport?

8

Which country won the World Team Squash Championships in 2007?

9

Who won ten consecutive men's British Open singles titles in the 1980s?

10

Which country will host the 2010 World Open Championships?

11

Who was British Open men's singles champion in 2008?

12

Who won the first professional World Open for men in 1976?

1

How many red balls are there in a frame?

2

Which cue-and-ball game was snooker mainly derived from?

3

What is the maximum break available on a snooker table?

4

Who compiled the fastest-ever maximum break?

5

How does a snooker ball "wipe its feet"?

6

In which year was the first snooker World Championship?

7

Who reigned as world champion from 1927 to 1940?

8

Which player was nicknamed "The Thai-Phoon"?

9

Who is the record-holder for breaks of 100 or more?

10

Who are the only two world champions not to have come from the UK?

11

Who is the only player to achieve a whitewash in the
Championship finals?

12

Who was World Snooker Champion in 2009?

OTHER INDIVIDUAL SPORTS
DARTS

1

What is the standard distance from which darts players may throw?

2

What is the lowest number of darts needed to finish a game of 501?

3

When was the first Embassy World Professional Championship held?

4

Who won it?

5

Which player was known as "The Milky Bar Kid"?

6

Who became BDO World Champion in 2009?

7

Who has won the world championship title most times?

8

Which player was nicknamed "The Menace"?

9

What is the name for the darts equivalent of "the yips"?

10

Which number on the board is "Annie's Room"?

11

In which year were darts first televised in Britain?

12

Who was the women's world champion from 2001 to 2007?

1

What was a "battledore" (the early badminton racquet) made of?

2

How high is a standard badminton net?

3

Before scoring changes in 2006, what was the winning total in a game?

4

Why is the game of "badminton" so called?

5

When were the first Badminton World Championships held?

6

Who has been All England men's singles champion most times?

7

What nationality was the great women's player Tonny Ahm?

8

How many goose feathers are used to make a professional shuttlecock?

9

Who holds the world speed record for a smash?

10

In which year did badminton become a competitive Olympic sport?

11

Which country won more than half the badminton medals at
the 2008 Games?

12

Who won gold in the 2008 Olympics men's singles?

OTHER INDIVIDUAL SPORTS
FENCING

1

Which are the three types of blade used in modern fencing?

2

What kind of equipment is the "plastron"?

3

Which great Italian left hander won 13 Olympic medals?

4

In which year were the World Championships first held?

5

What part of a foil is the "coquille"?

6

What are the limits of the valid target area in *épée* fighting?

7

Which country has won most Olympic women's fencing medals?

8

At which Olympics was the last single-stick competition?

9

How many medals did British men win in fencing at the 2008 Games?

10

Who won gold in the men's individual foil in the Beijing Olympics?

11

Which Hungarian won women's Olympic golds before and after
World War II?

12

Which city will host the 2010 World Fencing Championships?

1

What is the name of the oldest surviving curling stone?

2

What is the standard maximum weight of a curling stone?

3

What is the circular target curlers aim at?

4

Why is this sedate sport known as "The Roaring Game"?

5

What is special about the Royal Montreal Curling Club?

6

In which year was curling first included in the Winter Olympics?

7

Which team won the men's Olympic title in 2006?

8

Who captained Britain's women gold medallists at the 2002 Olympics?

9

What is the maximum length of a standard curling "sheet"?

10

What shape are the top and bottom of a curling stone?

11

Which team won gold at the 2009 World Men's Championships?

12

Curling stones are made of granite from which Scottish island?

OTHER INDIVIDUAL SPORTS
WRESTLING

1

Which English and French kings had a wrestling match in 1520?

2

What is the main limit imposed on Graeco-Roman wrestlers?

3

In which year did women wrestlers first compete in the Olympics?

4

What is the longest recorded modern wrestling match?

5

What, in freestyle wrestling, is a "grapevine"?

6

How many wrestlers took part in the 1896 Olympic Games?

7

Who won the gold medal at that Games?

8

Who was the last Briton to win an Olympic wrestling medal?

9

Where is the passivity zone?

10

How many wrestling medals did Britain win at the 2008 Olympics?

11

Who won gold in the men's super-heavyweight Graeco-Roman in 2008?

12

Who starred in the 2008 film *The Wrestler*?

OTHER INDIVIDUAL SPORTS
SHOOTING

. . . .

1

At which Olympics was the shooting of pigeons included?

2

Which are the three shotgun events in competitive shooting?

3

Who was the first (and last) woman to win a mixed-sex Olympic
shooting event?

4

Which French pistol champion founded the modern Olympics?

5

Which Hungarian won Olympic golds after switching from right-
to left-handed?

6

What distance are targets set in Olympic rifle events?

7

What is the greatest number of shooting events held at a single Olympics?

8

In which two Olympic years were there no shooting events?

9

Who scored a perfect 400 in the women's air rifle event at Beijing 2008?

10

What first was achieved by Abhinav Bindra at the 2008 Olympics?

11

Which two shooting golds at the 2008 Games were won by US competitors?

12

Who twice broke the men's Olympic double trap record at Beijing?

1

Where were the first world weightlifting championships held in 1891?

2

What are the two recognized lifts in weightlifting?

3

Who won the first women's superheavyweight gold at the 2000 Olympics?

4

What nationality is champion lifter Hossein Rezazadeh?

5

Which Russian set an amazing 80 world records in the 1970s?

6

What is the heaviest clean-and-jerk of all time?

7

Who was the first lifter to win golds at three different Olympic Games?

8

Which great US lifter was unbeaten between 1938 and 1953?

9

What, in powerlifting, is a "dead lift"?

10

In the event of a tie in weightlifting, who wins?

11

Which country won most weightlifting golds at the 2008 Olympics?

12

What tragedy befell Janos Baranyai at the 2008 Olympics?

OTHER INDIVIDUAL SPORTS
DIVING

. . . .

1

How high is the highest Olympic diving platform?

2

Which new diving discipline was adopted for the 2000 Olympics?

3

In which year was diving first included in the Olympics?

4

Which diving event was discontinued after the 1904 Games?

5

Who won gold for the women's platform dive at the 2008 Olympics?

6

Which 14 year-old represented Britain at the 2008 Olympics?

7

Who is the only Olympic diver to win back-to-back 3m and 10m golds?

8

Which pair won Britain's last Olympic diving medal?

9

Which country won most golds at the 2007 World Aquatics
Championships?

10

How many diving medals did the USA win at the 2008 Olympics?

11

Who won gold in the men's 10m dive in the Beijing Games?

12

What kind of dive is an "armstand"?

1

What does the Japanese word *judo* mean in English?

2

What is the name of the winning score for a perfect move?

3

Who founded judo in the 19th-century?

4

What is the name of the white uniforms used in judo?

5

In which year did men's judo become an Olympic event?

6

Which Briton was four times women's world champion in the 1980s?

7

Which Goon was once President of the London Judo Society?

8

Which European prince is a 1st dan black belt?

9

Who was the first ever World Judo Champion in 1956?

10

Which country other than Japan has headed a Championship medals table?

11

Who was the first non-Japanese to win a world judo title?

12

What happens when a referee calls "Sono-mamma"?

OTHER INDIVIDUAL SPORTS
OTHER MARTIAL ARTS

1

What does the Japanese name *aikido* mean literally in English?

2

Which military class in medieval Japan developed jujitsu?

3

Which team won five successive golds in the World Karate Championships?

4

What is the Japanese name for a hammer fist strike in karate?

5

Which karate style is used by film star Jean-Claude Van Damme?

6

In karate, what is a "sensei"?

7

In which Japanese martial art is a bamboo sword used?

8

In which martial art was Kash "The Flash" Gill a British professional?

9

Who became men's world superheavyweight kickboxing champion in 2007?

10

In which country was kung fu developed?

11

Which Chinese kung fu champion made his screen debut in *Lethal Weapon 4*?

12

Which Korean form of karate became an Olympic sport in 2000?

OTHER INDIVIDUAL SPORTS
ICE SKATING

1

When was the first World Allround Speed Skating Championships for men?

2

Which country has since won most golds at this competition ?

3

What, in skating, is a "camel spin"?

4

Which skater won six women's Olympic and World titles during the 1980s?

5

Who holds the men's speed skating world record for 1,500m?

6

How many speed skating world records are held by Canada's Cindy Klassen?

7

When did Torvill and Dean win their Olympic ice dance gold medal?

8

Which Briton won gold in men's figure skating at the 1976 Olympics?

9

Who was Irina Rodnina's pairs partner in six World Championships?

10

Who won gold in women's figure skating at the 2006 Winter Olympics?

11

How many feet are involved in a "choctaw" or a "mohawk"?

12

Who is the youngest Olympic figure skating gold medallist ever?

1

In archery, what is the "upshot"?

2

Who holds the record for most All-England badminton titles?

3

Who has been World Indoor Bowls Champion five times since 1999?

4

Which Irish boxing champion's father appeared in the Eurovision Song Contest?

5

Who sensationally defeated Mike Tyson in 1990?

6

In curling, where is the "tee"?

7

How high is a darts bull from the floor?

8

What feature does a "carom" billiards table lack?

9

In darts, what score is a "madhouse"?

10

In which year was ice dance first contested at the Olympics?

11

Who won 2 silver and 2 women's judo golds at Olympics from 1992 to 2004?

12

What name is given to the novice rank in karate?

OTHER INDIVIDUAL SPORTS
MIXED BAG (2)

1

Which country hosted the 2007 Kickboxing World Championships?

2

Which form of kung fu is judged on style alone?

3

Which country is the overall leader of the summer Olympics medals table?

4

Where was the venue of the very first Paralympic Summer Games in 1952?

5

What was the real name of pool legend Minnesota Fats?

6

Who was the 2009 World Rackets singles champion?

7

Which country won the first World Roller Hockey Championships in 1936?

8

What are the "three positions" in smallbore rifle shooting?

9

Which snooker star was known as "The Romford Robot" or "Interesting"?

10

What is the longest distance for a standard speed-skating race?

11

Which skater won China's first-ever gold at a Winter Olympics?

12

What colour of dot denotes the fastest type of squash ball?

ANSWERS
FOOTBALL: HOME

....

ENGLAND

....

1. 35; 2. None; 3. Graeme Le Saux; 4. Austria; 5. Six; 6. Mexico;
7. 1872; 8. Slovakia; 9. Owen Hargreaves; 10. 2000;
11. England, 6-3; 12. 1958

....

TECHNICAL TERMS

....

1. Keeper may not handle the ball in the penalty box if passed by
a team-mate; 2. Libero; 3. Goal scored in extra time which does not
decide the game immediately; 4. Nutmeg; 5. The goal netting;
6. Futsal; 7. The Bosman Ruling; 8. The Bundesliga; 9. Corner arcs;
10. Association football; 11. The far post; 12. The Horseshoe

....

NAME THE YEAR (1)

....

1. 1998; 2. 1949; 3. 1973; 4. 1923; 5. 1985; 6. 1969; 7. 1964; 8. 2008;
9. 1978; 10. 1966; 11. 1984; 12. 1903

....

FA CUP (1)

....

1. Bury, 6-0 (1903); 2. David Nish; 3. West Ham and QPR;
4. Roberto di Matteo; 5. Bill Brown; 6. Tranmere Rovers;
7. Manchester United (11); 8. Harry Cursham, Notts County (49);
9. Most goals in a single game (9); 10. They held it during World War
Two, when the competition was suspended; 11. Louis Saha, Everton,
25 seconds (2009); 12. Seven

....

ANSWERS
FOOTBALL: HOME

··

RECORD BREAKERS

··

1. Alan Shearer (260); 2. David James (537); 3. Kenny Dalglish (102);
4. Manchester United (18); 5. Most League goals (433);
6. Dixie Dean (60); 7. Manchester City, 10 (2006/7); 8. Arsenal
(2003/4); 9. Peter Shilton, 1,005; 10. Chelsea (95); 11. Ian Rush (28);
12. Ryan Giggs (11)

··

GOALSCORERS & GOALKEEPERS

··

1. 4 seconds, Jim Fryatt (Bradford), 1964; 2. Chris Nicholl (Aston
Villa); 3. Chesterfield; 4. 23; 5. Gary Sprake; 6. Northampton Town;
7. Teacher; 8. Edwin van der Sar (Manchester United),
14 games, 2008/9; 9. 1956/7 and 1958/9 (103 in each);
10. Xabi Alonso, Liverpool v Newcastle (2006), 210ft (64m);
11. Paul Robinson (2007), 289ft (88m); 12. Since 1970

··

NAME THE YEAR (2)

··

1. 1986; 2. 1921; 3. 1994; 4. 1998; 5. 1991; 6. 1976; 7. 1976; 8. 1998;
9. 1939; 10. 1928; 11. 2005; 12. 1995

··

QUOTES: WHO SAID...? (1)

··

1. Alex Ferguson; 2. Alf Ramsey; 3. Bill Shankly; 4. Bill Shankly;
5. Brian Clough; 6. Graeme Souness; 7. Berti Vogts; 8. John Bond;
9. Jackie Charlton; 10. Dave Bassett; 11. Matt Busby;
12. Bill Shankly

··

ANSWERS
FOOTBALL: HOME

....

THE FOOTBALL LEAGUE
....

1. Doncaster Rovers; 2. Phil Neale; 3. Eric Cantona;
4. Halifax Town; 5. Crewe Alexandra; 6. Chesterfield;
7. Carlisle United; 8. Manchester City; 9. 1962;
10. Wolverhampton Wanderers and Burnley; 11. Derby County and
Nottingham Forest; 12. Wycombe Wanderers

REFEREES
....

1. Diego Simeone 2. David Batty; 3. Wendy Toms; 4. Eight miles;
5. He refereed the first FA Cup Final; 6. 1878; 7. Mike Dean;
8. He was sent off; 9. Paul Durkin; 10. Blew the whistle five minutes
early; 11. Peter Willis (1985); 12. Allowed an offside goal which cost
Leeds a victory

NAME THE YEAR (3)
....

1. 1999; 2. 1935; 3. 1989; 4. 1912; 5. 1977; 6. 1923;
7. 1956 (Stanley Matthews); 8. 1976; 9. 1994; 10. 1966; 11. 1953;
12. 1959

THE PREMIERSHIP
....

1. 1992; 2. Manchester United (11); 3. Derby County (2007/8);
4. Ryan Giggs (523); 5. Alan Shearer and Cristiano Ronaldo (31);
6. Most red cards (8); 7. None; 8. Roy Evans; 9. Michael Owen;
10. Swindon Town; 11. Mauricio Taricco; 12. Peter Swales

ANSWERS
FOOTBALL: HOME

SEEING RED

1. Kevin Keegan; 2. 20 (Sportivo Ameliano v General Caballero, Paraguay, 1993); 3. Antonio Rattin; 4. Argentina; 5. Graeme Hogg and Craig Levein; 6. Trevor Hockey; 7. Emmanuel Petit; 8. John Murray; 9. Mal Donaghy; 10. Lee Bowyer and Danny Mills; 11. Eric Abidal (Barcelona); 12. Joe Jordan

FA CUP (2)

1. Norman Whiteside; 2. Nine (Arthur Kinnaird); 3. 731; 4. Aston Villa v Sunderland (1913), 120,081; 5. 1922; 6. Leicester City; 7. Peterborough; 8. All were won by the away team; 9. Martin Buchan; 10. Mark Hughes; 11. Joe Royle; 12. Ashley Cole

MANCHESTER AND MERSEYSIDE

1. 236; 2 .Peter Schmeichel; 3. Dave Sexton; 4. 48; 5. 1965; 6. Alan Oakes; 7. Three; 8. 229; 9. Ian Callaghan; 10. Duncan Ferguson; 11. Bill Kenwright; 12. Aston Villa

LONDON CLUBS

1. Gordon Jago; 2. Michael Marks; 3. Walsall; 4. 1991; 5. Charley Preedy; 6. Freddy Ljungberg; 7. Bobby Campbell; 8. Ian Hamilton; 9. Five – Walter Winterbottom, Joe Mercer, Ron Greenwood, Terry Venables, Glenn Hoddle; 10. 1961; 11. John White; 12. Glenn Hoddle

ANSWERS

....

ODDITIES (1)

....

1. Oxford United; 2. Eric Cantona; 3. A turnip; 4. Stoke City;
5. Kevin Keegan; 6. Meadowbank Thistle; 7. San Marino;
8. Kidderminster Harriers; 9. Bert Trautmann (1956);
10. Total Network Solutions; 11. 1977; 12. 436ft 4ins (133m)

....

SCOTLAND

....

1. Czechoslovakia; 2. 26; 3. New Zealand; 4. Huddersfield Town;
5. Paul Lambert; 6. Don Hutchison; 7. It is not an independent
member of the IOC; 8. Partick; 9. 1872; 10. 1954; 11. Alex Ferguson;
12. Kenny Dalglish and Denis Law (30)

....

ALL ROUNDERS

....

1. Andy Goram; 2. Arsenal; 3. Ian Botham; 4. Arthur Milton;
5. Stan Mortensen; 6. C.B.Fry; 7. Max Woosnam; 8. After a day's
cricket with Leicestershire, he played an evening game for
Doncaster Rovers; 9. Frank Sugg (1862-1933); 10. Vinnie Jones;
11. David Beckham; 12. Terry Venables

....

QUOTES: WHO SAID...? (2)

....

1. Victoria Beckham; 2. Eric Hall (agent); 3. Brian Clough;
4. Queen Elizabeth II; 5. Danny Blanchflower; 6. Bill Shankly;
7. Roy Keane; 8. Carlos Queiroz; 9. Gianfranco Zola; 10. Craig Brown;
11. Ian Wright; 12. Stuart Pearce

....

ANSWERS

FOOTBALL: HOME

··

ODDITIES (2)

··

1. Rotherham United; 2. Charlie George;
3. Oxford United and Reading; 4. Mickey Walsh;
5. Accrington Stanley; 6. Manchester City; 7. Huddersfield Town;
8. Petr Cech (Chelsea), 2004/5; 9. Gordon Brown; 10. Scotland;
11. Rangers; 12. Hull City

··

WHERE DO THEY PLAY?

··

1. Huddersfield Town; 2. Tannadice Park; 3. Millwall; 4. Glenavon;
5. Stenhousemuir; 6. Norwich City; 7. Racecourse Ground;
8. Brandywell; 9. Glebe Park (Brechin City); 10. Hartlepool United;
11. East End Park; 12. Dover Athletic

··

MANAGERS

··

1. 1977; 2. Rotherham United; 3. 1977; 4. 1967; 5. Bobby Moore;
6. Oldham Athletic; 7. Walter Winterbottom; 8. Matt Busby;
9. Leroy Rosenior, 10 minutes (2007); 10. Brian Clough (4);
11. Willie Bell; 12. F.C.Porto

··

ANCIENT HISTORY

··

1. 1863; 2. Jules Rimet; 3. The Romans; 4. Edward III; 5. Florence;
6. The FA Cup; 7. Kirkwall, Orkneys; 8. 1928; 9. Women's football;
10. Alexander Watson Hutton; 11. Uruguay and Argentina (1901);
12. Egypt, 1920

··

ANSWERS
TENNIS

RECORD BREAKERS (1)

1. Bill Scanlon (1983); 2. Steffi Graf (32 minutes, 1988);
3. Fabrice Santoro v Arnaud Clement (6hrs 33 minutes, 2004);
4. John McEnroe (147); 5. Martina Navratilova (167); 6. Four;
7. 2001; 8. Bjorn Borg (89.8%); 9. Ken Rosewall (23); 10. Martina
Navratilova (74); 11. Maud Watson (1884); 12. Jean Borotra (223)

NICKNAMES: WHO WERE...?

1. Jean Borotra; 2. Maureen Connolly; 3. Rod Laver; 4. R.A.Gonzales;
5. Tom Okker; 6. Jane Bartkowicz; 7. Wendy Turnbull;
8. Roy Emerson; 9. Venus Williams; 10. Mark Philippoussis;
11. Gertrude Moran; 12. Helen Wills Moody

NAME THE CITY: WHERE ARE...?

1. New York; 2. Shanghai; 3. Melbourne; 4. Paris; 5. Bangkok;
6. Zurich; 7. Melbourne; 8. Kolkata; 9. Montreal; 10. London;
11. Zagreb; 12. Antwerp

ANCIENT HISTORY

1. The palm of the hand; 2. Real (royal) tennis; 3. *Henry V*;
4. French Revolution; 5. 1873; 6. From "l'oeuf" (French for egg),
referring to an egg-shaped score; 7. Croquet;
8. Mary Ewing Outerbridge; 9. 1881; 10. 1905; 11. USA and Great
Britain; 12. The International Tennis Federation

ANSWERS
TENNIS

....

TECHNICAL TERMS

....

1. A set won without dropping a point; 2. The right side;
3. A set won 6-0; 4. A shot played off the racket frame;
5. Pete Sampras; 6. Between the tramlines; 7. The return of a
difficult shot; 8. A shot with little or no spin; 9. A serve with a lot of
spinning which bounces high; 10. Two doubles players standing on
the same side of the court at the start of a point; 11. Women's Tennis
Association; 12. Straight at the opponent's body

....

QUOTES: WHO SAID...?

....

1. Billie-Jean King; 2. Pete Sampras; 3. Andy Murray;
4. Ana Invanovic; 5. Rafael Nadal; 6. Jean Borotra; 7. Martina Hingis;
8. J.M.Barrie; 9. George Bernard Shaw; 10. Blaise Pascal;
11. Pat Rafter; 12. Viginia Graham

....

THE GRAND SLAM

....

1. Australian Open, French Open, Wimbledon, US Open; 2. 1938;
3. Rod Laver; 4. 1962 and 1969; 5. Australian Open; 6. Red clay;
7. The Olympic championship; 8. Five; 9. US Open; 10. The Small
Slam; 11. Frank Sedgman and Ken McGregor (1951); 12. She has won
Grand Slams in two categories (singles and mixed doubles)

....

THE DAVIS CUP

....

1. USA (32); 2. Dwight F Davis; 3. India; 4. Mohammed Akhtar
Hossain (Bangladesh), 13 years 326 days; 5. Nicola Pietrangeli (164);
6. 1927; 7. Five; 8. 16; 9. 137; 10. Five; 11. Italy; 12. 1936

....

ANSWERS
TENNIS

···

RECORD BREAKERS (2)

···

1. Bill Tilden (163mph, 262.8 km/h) (1931); 2. Lottie Dod (1887);
3. Margaret Court (21); 4. 1984; 5. The VW Grand Prix Open Amateur
Championship, 321,000 (UK, 1984); 6. Arthur Gore, 41 years 182 days;
7. 48 hours 15 minutes (Brian Jahrsdoerfer & Michel Lavoie and
Peter Okpokpo & Warner Tse, 2006); 8. Venus Williams, (127mph,
204.3 km/h) (1998); 9. 15,674 shots (Rob Peterson and Ray Miller,
2000); 10. Ivo Karlovic, 55 (2009); 11. Martina Navratilova,
9 women's doubles (US Open); 12. George VI (1926)

NAME THE YEAR

···

1. 1925; 2. 1948; 3. 2001; 4. 2006; 5. 1969; 6. 1953 and 1972; 7. 2005;
8. 1928; 9. 1988; 10. 1970; 11. 1905 (May Sutton); 12. 2000

WIMBLEDON (1)

···

1. 1907; 2. Two – Arthur Gore and Fred Perry; 3. Five; 4. 1940;
5. Althea Gibson; 6. 1968; 7. 81 players boycotted the event after
Nikki Pilic was suspended; 8. Jan Kodes; 9. Boris Becker;
10. Bjorn Borg (5 successive men's singles titles); 11. 1984; 12. 1993

WIMBLEDON (2)

···

1. They were at the ceremony to test the new retractable roof;
2. Four; 3. Reigning champions no longer had a bye to the final;
4. 19; 5. Ball boys and girls; 6. £850,000; 7. Todd Woodbridge (9);
8. Suzanne Lenglen (5); 9. Goran Ivanisevic (125th); 10. 2008 men's
singles (Roger Federer v Rafael Nadal), 4 hours 48 mins;
11. Martina Navratilova (326); 12. Laura Robson

ANSWERS
TENNIS

....

37 THE US OPEN

....

1. USTA Billie Jean King National Tennis Center;
2. There are tie-breaks in final sets; 3. Philadelphia; 4. $1.5 million;
5. Bill Tilden (16); 6. Tracey Austin, 16 years 8 months;
7. Andy Murray; 8. Twice; 9. Ellen Hansell; 10. Four;
11. Cara Black and Leander Paes; 12. Chris Evert

....

38 THE FRENCH OPEN

....

1. A French World War One flying ace; 2. 1925; 3. Once (2009);
4. Rod Laver; 5. Max Decugis (29); 6. Suzanne Lenglen (4);
7. Michael Chang, 17 years and 3 months; 8. She was the first non-seed to win a singles title; 9. Anabel Medina and Virginia Ruano;
10. H Briggs; 11. 1891; 12. Dinara Safina

....

39 THE AUSTRALIAN OPEN

....

1. 1987; 2. The first time singles and doubles titles have been won by siblings; 3. Plexicushion Prestige; 4. 1912; 5. Flinders Park; 6. None;
7. The date was moved from December to January of the following year, thereby missing a year; 8. Margaret Court (11);
9. Adrian Quist (13); 10. Ken Rosewall, 18 years 2 months;
11. Ken Rosewall, 37 years 8 months; 12. Dinara Safina

....

40 GREAT MATCHES – IN WHICH YEAR DID...?

....

1. 1926; 2. 1958; 3. 1980; 4. 1969; 5. 1927; 6. 1937; 7. 1964; 8. 2008;
9. 1975; 10. 1988; 11. 1989; 12. 2001

....

ANSWERS
TENNIS

FAMOUS PLAYERS – MEN

1. Donald Budge; 2. Bill Tilden; 3. Jack Kramer; 4. Rod Laver;
5. 41; 6. 41; 7. Jean Borotra, Jacques Brugnon, Henri Cochet and
René Lacoste; 8. Roger Federer; 9. Five; 10. 17; 11. John McEnroe;
12. Rafael Nadal

FAMOUS PLAYERS – WOMEN

1. Steffi Graf; 2. Evonne Goolagong (1971); 3. Suzanne Lenglen;
4. The first woman to complete a Grand Slam; 5. Margaret Court;
6. Helen Wills Moody playing tennis; 7. Czechoslovakia;
8. Billie Jean King; 9. Hazel Hotchkiss Wightman; 10. Virginia Wade;
11. Justine Henin; 12. Chris Evert (90%)

OLYMPIC TENNIS

1. Yes; 2. 1924; 3. 1988; 4. Great Britain (44); 5. One;
6. Reginald Doherty (4); 7. Russia; 8. 2004; 9. Beijing; 10. Serena and
Venus Williams; 11. Bronze in the men's singles; 12. USA (12)

WHO WAS THE MOST FAMOUS PARTNER OF...?

1. Bob Hewitt; 2. Mark Woodforde; 3. Peter McNamara;
4. Jelena Jankovitch; 5. Pam Shriver; 6. Billie Jean King;
7. John Newcombe; 8. Jana Novotna; 9. Roy Emerson;
10. Frank Sedgman; 11. Serena Williams; 12. John McEnroe

······························

CYCLING (1)

······························

1. 8 seconds (Greg LeMond 1989); 2. 1839; 3. Paris (1868);
4. Belgium; 5. 1893; 6. 1903; 7. Maurice Garin; 8. A group distance
race with set sprint periods; 9. Chris Boardman; 10. Arnaud Tournant
(58.875 seconds); 11. Eddy Merckx; 12. Vuelta a España

CYCLING (2)

······························

1. Criteriums; 2. The Race Across America; 3. Marco Pantani;
4. 2005; 5. Roubaix; 6. 1896; 7. Ronde van Vlaanderen; 8. Adelaide;
9. Allan Davis; 10. France (40); 11. Nicole Cooke; 12. 14

CYCLING (3)

······························

1. Eugène Christophe; 2. Bernard Hinault; 3. A time trial;
4. A very low gear; 5. Men's Cross Country Mountain Biking;
6. Poland; 7. Australia (10); 8. Mario Cipollini; 9. A 2km track sprint
for 6-8 riders; 10. Chris Hoy; 11. Women's Individual Sprint;
12. Damjan Zabovnik (54.1miles, 87.123km)

CYCLING (4)

······························

1. Miguel Indurain; 2. Rider's water bottle; 3. Ondrej Sosenka
(30.8miles, 49.7km); 4. Carlos Sastre; 5. 1953; 6. Richard Virenque
(7); 7. Jacques Anquetil; 8. 445; 9. Jeannie Longo-Ciprelli;
10. When riding at his or her physical limit;
11. Djamolodine Abdoujaparov; 12. Varese, Italy

. . . .

HORSE RACING (1)

. . . .

1. Newmarket, Long Island, NY; 2. 1665; 3. Siena, Italy;
4. Newmarket; 5. Five; 6. West Australian; 7. The 2,000 Guineas;
8. Shergar (10 lengths); 9. 1861; 10. 25,095-1; 11. Jem Mason;
12. Tony McCoy

. . . .

HORSE RACING (2)

. . . .

1. National Hunt race for horses who have not competed in flat races
or over NH jumps; 2. Arkle; 3. Seb Saunders and Jamie Spence;
4. Red Rum; 5. 66 (1929); 6. Mr Light (1:31.41); 7. Affirmed (1978);
8. The Preakness Stakes; 9. Co. Kildare; 10. Lester Piggott;
11. Australia; 12. Captain Martin Becher (after falling in the water in
1839: his name was given to Becher's Brook)

. . . .

HORSE RACING (3)

. . . .

1. His 3,000th winner; 2. A favourite bookies don't expect to win;
3. Willie Shoemaker; 4. Golden Miller; 5. Edward VII; 6. 40;
7. Lester Piggott; 8. Japan; 9. Windsor Slipper (1942);
10. Belmont Park; 11. Jenny Pitman; 12. Vincent O'Brien

. . . .

HORSE RACING (4)

. . . .

1. 26; 2. 100-30; 3. 2008; 4. Dubai World Cup ($6m);
5. Petrone (3:18.0); 6. Red Splash; 7. 1928; 8. 12; 9. Kentucky Derby;
10. One-and-a-half miles (2.4km); 11. 1971; 12. Earth Summit

. . . .

ANSWERS
RACING & SPEED

··

SWIMMING (1)

··

1. 1972; 2. Johnny Weissmuller and Clarence "Buster" Crabbe;
3. Frederick Bousquet (20.94); 4. Marleen Veldhuis (6); 5. 50m;
6. 1844; 7. Captain Matthew Webb (1875); 8. Alfred Hajos; 9. 1912;
10. A perfect entry with little splash; 11. Dawn Fraser;
12. Gertrude Ederle (1926)

··

SWIMMING (2)

··

1. Kosuke Kitajima; 2. Individual Medley; 3. Michael Gross;
4. Rebecca Adlington; 5. One leg extended upwards, the other drawn
into the chest; 6. None; 7. 1973; 8. Kristin Otto (6); 9. 72 days;
10. USA (214); 11. 1900; 12. Beijing

··

SWIMMING (3)

··

1. 1976; 2. Six; 3. Zimbabwean; 4. 1956; 5. The 200m obstacle race;
6. Aaron Peirsol; 7. "Eric the Eel"; 8. Front crawl; 9. Swimming most
of the first length under water (after David Berkoff);
10. Inge de Bruijn; 11. Shane Gould; 12. Shanghai, China

··

MOTOR RACING (1)

··

1. 1887; 2. One; 3. Automobile Club de France; 4. 1901;
5. Giuseppe Farina; 6. 1950; 7. A team's spare car; 8. Jack Brabham;
9. Guy Smith (2003); 10. 0.043 of a second (Al Unser 1992);
11. Tom Kristensen; 12. 91

··

ANSWERS
RACING & SPEED

· ·

MOTOR RACING (2)

· ·

1. Australia; 2. Stock cars; 3. 1973; 4. Ferrari; 5. Nurburgring;
6. Stirling Moss; 7. Alain Prost; 8. Juan Fangio;
9. The track is slippery; 10. Sebastien Loeb; 11. Monaco 1933;
12. Mercedes and Auto Union

MOTOR RACING (3)

· ·

1. 1950; 2. Silverstone; 3. India; 4. Vanwall; 5. 1980; 6. Jacky Ickx;
7. Steve McQueen; 8. Jim Clark; 9. Four (Monaco 1966);
10. Helio Castroneves; 11. Lewis Hamilton; 12. Louis Meyer

MOTORCYCLING

· ·

1. 1907; 2. Sweden; 3. John Surtees; 4. Ivan Mauger;
5. A succession of hillocks or bumps; 6. Valentino Rossi; 7. 1200cc;
8. Troy Bayliss; 9. 500cc Champion; 10. Suzuki and Yamaha;
11. Snowmobiles; 12. Wembley Stadium

ROWING

· ·

1. Doggett's Coat and Badge; 2. 1829; 3. A small fin fixed at the stern
end of a boat; 4. 1984; 5. Lake Bled (Slovenia); 6. USA (3);
7. The weather was too bad; 8. Elisabeta Lipa (8); 9. Olaf Tufte;
10. Heavyweight double sculls and coxless four; 11. Coxswain;
12. Benjamin Spock

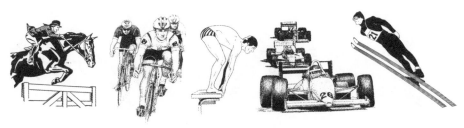

ANSWERS
RACING & SPEED

....

SAILING

....

1. 1851; 2. A harbour race round buoys; 3. Ellen MacArthur;
4. Chay Blyth; 5. Australia II; 6. 1983; 7. A small craft with a keel and
3 sails; 8. Michel Desjoyeaux; 9. Robin Knox-Johnston;
10. Edward Heath; 11. 57 days (Francis Joyon); 12. 3.6m (Serge Testa)

....

EQUESTRIAN

....

1. Lepping; 2. Four; 3. Lexington, Kentucky, USA; 4. Raimondo D'Inzeo;
5. A competition in which a horse jumps very high obstacles;
6. Germany (21); 7. Lucinda Green; 8. Aachen; 9. A slow trot in which
the horse's neck is arched, the head is vertical and the hindquarters
are lowered; 10. Dressage, eventing and jumping;
11. Male cavalry officers; 12. Hong Kong

....

SKIING

....

1. Where the slope flattens out; 2. 1936; 3. Anja Paerson; 4. 1985;
5. Christl Kranz; 6. Distance and style; 7. Too little snow;
8. 156mph (251.4km/h) (Simone Origone); 9. Antoine Deneriaz;
10. Turin, Italy; 11. One downhill and two slaloms; 12. Sochi, Russia

....

MIXED BAG

....

1. The Gordon Bennett Cup; 2. Jamaica; 3. A fast turn using the
paddle as pivot; 4. Dragster (drag racing car); 5. Greyhound racing;
6. Sonia Henie; 7. Sledge; 8. Gee Atherton; 9. Switzerland;
10. Speed skydiving; 11. Iditarod; 12. 1984

....

. . . .

RECORD BREAKERS

. . . .

1. Daisuke Ohata (69); 2. Doug Howlett (49); 3. Michael Lynagh (911);
4. George Lindsay (5) 1887; 5. 80 points, by England v Italy, 2001;
6. Jonny Wilkinson (1,099); 7. 18 seconds, by Elton Flatley, Australia
v Romania, 2003; 8. Most tests refereed (44); 9. Scotland and England;
10. Jason Leonard (22); 11. Jannie de Beer (5); 12. Jonah Lomu (15)

NICKNAMES – WHICH TEAMS ARE KNOWN AS...?

. . . .

1. Swansea; 2. Uruguay; 3. Taranaki; 4. Leicester; 5. Tonga;
6. Canada; 7. Japan; 8. Western Province; 9. South Africa;
10. New Zealand women's team; 11. Gloucester; 12. London Irish

TECHNICAL TERMS

. . . .

1. The area behind the scrum half or set-piece;
2. A high up-and-under kick; 3. Left; 4. Move in which ball-carrier is
shielded by a team-mate: it is illegal; 5. The forwards;
6. Players drink after the game; 7. To penalize someone; 8. The backs;
9. The players fight; 10. Fly half; 11. Scrum half and fly half;
12. First and second rows in the scrum

ANCIENT HISTORY

. . . .

1. Rugby (obviously); 2. William Webb Ellis; 3. Guy's Hospital FC;
4. 1871; 5. Frederick Stokes; 6. No points; 7. It had to be oval; 8. 1895;
9. USA; 10. 1928; 11. New Zealand and Australia; 12. 1947

ANSWERS
RUGBY UNION

··

RUGBY GROUNDS

··

1. Bath; 2. Kingsholm; 3. Rome; 4. Wales; 5. The Stoop; 6. Dublin;
7. Sydney; 8. Carisbrook; 9. Newlands; 10. Stade de France;
11. Argentina; 12. 1925

··

QUOTES: WHO SAID...?

··

1. Ray Gravell; 2. Elizabeth Taylor; 3. Will Carling;
4. Pierre Berbizier; 5. The All Blacks (their motto); 6. Gordon Brown;
7. Graham Mourie; 8. Eddie Jones; 9. Henry Blaha;
10. Steve Smith (to Bill Beaumont, of a female streaker);
11. Gavin Hastings; 12. Jean-Pierre Rives

··

NAME THE YEAR

··

1. 1823; 2. 1987; 3. 1845; 4. 1996; 5. 1999; 6. 1973; 7. 1998; 8. 1967;
9. 1995; 10. 1948; 11. 1995; 12. 2000

··

THE SIX (OR FIVE) NATIONS

··

1. England (12); 2. Calcutta Cup; 3. Giuseppe Garibaldi Trophy;
4. Triple Crown; 5. 1959; 6. 2003; 7. Mike Gibson (56);
8. Ian Smith (24); 9. England (229 in 2001);
10. Ireland and France (36); 11. Brian O'Driscoll and Riki Flutey (4);
12. Ronan O'Gara (51)

··

ANSWERS
RUGBY UNION

....

THE TRI-NATIONS

....

1. 1903; 2. Australia; 3. Fiji, Samoa and Tonga; 4. Jonah Lomu;
5. Christian Cullen (16); 6. Percy Montgomery (210); 7. One;
8. Argentina; 9. Four; 10. Four or more; 11. 1921; 12. Nine

....

WORLD CUP

....

1. 20; 2. Australia and New Zealand; 3. One; 4. Joel Stransky;
5. Australia; 6. To the semi-finals; 7. 48; 8. New Zealand;
9. Grant Fox (126 in 1987); 10. 142 points (Aus v Namibia, 2003);
11. Mike Catt (36 years 33 days); 12. Jonny Wilkinson

....

ALL BLACKS

....

1. 1905; 2. 1956; 3. A silver fern; 4. The *haka* usually performed by
the All Blacks; 5. "The Invincibles"; 6. 17 matches (1965-70);
7. France; 8. "Pinetree"; 9. Sean Fitzpatrick (92);
10. Jonah Lomu (19 years 45 days); 11. Andrew Mehrtens (967);
12. Most tries in a calendar year (17)

....

THE BRITISH AND IRISH LIONS

....

1. South Africa; 2. 1927; 3. Ronnie Dawson; 4. Carwyn James;
5. 1989; 6. 1974; 7. Willie John McBride; 8. It was the bicentenary of
the French Revolution; 9. 20 points (1993); 10. South Africa (46);
11. Australia; 12. Ceylon (now Sri Lanka)

....

ANSWERS
RUGBY UNION / LEAGUE

. . . .

THE SPRINGBOKS

. . . .

1. The protea; 2. 1891; 3. 134–3 v Uruguay (2005); 4. 15-12;
5. They were banned because of South Africa's apartheid regime;
6. Both were Maoris (and thus considered coloured); 7. British Lions;
8. England; 9. Chester Williams; 10. Percy Mongomery (102);
11. Joost van der Westhuizen (38); 12. Jake White

. . . .

THE WALLABIES

. . . .

1. 64; 2. Twice; 3. George Gregan (139); 4. 1899; 5. 12;
6. The Cook Cup; 7. 8-53 v South Africa (2008); 8. John Eales;
9. Twice; 10. Rod MacQueen; 11. 1908; 12. Scrum half

. . . .

GREAT PLAYERS

. . . .

1. J P R.Williams; 2. Lock; 3. 27; 4. François Pienaar; 5. Philippe Sella;
6. Sean Fitzpatrick; 7. Serge Blanco; 8. 1999; 9. Gareth Edwards;
10. Rory Underwood (49); 11. Colin Meads; 12. Alexander Obolensky

. . . .

RECORD BREAKERS

. . . .

1. Ellery Hanley (3); 2. St Helens; 3. Keith Senior (156);
4. Brisbane Broncos (3); 5. 76-4 v Russia (2000); 6. 66,000 (1995);
7. George Smith (New Zealand); 8. Jason Taylor (11); 9. Great Britain;
10. Mick Cronin (112); 11. Australia (9); 12. Wigan Warriors (17)

. . . .

ANSWERS
RUGBY LEAGUE

....

WHICH NATIONAL TEAMS ARE CALLED...?

....

1. Australia; 2. Russia; 3. USA; 4. Papua New Guinea; 5. France;
6. Lebanon; 7. New Zealand; 8. Ireland; 9. Fiji; 10. Scotland;
11. Tonga; 12. Serbia

....

TECHNICAL TERMS

....

1. Drop goal; 2. To pick up the ball after a restart; 3. An extra tackle
awarded before the set six for a knock-on or forward pass; 4. Behind
one optional player to another; 5. The line taken by a player to take a
pass inside from the ball carrier who is running across the face of the
defence; 6. By getting more players to the ball than the opposition;
7. When a ball carrier stops play though not properly tackled;
8. Ball kicked along the ground; 9. A kick deliberately skewed right
or left; 10. When the ball strikes a player's head; 11. Crash ball;
12. The act of running the ball on the 5th tackle instead of kicking

....

ANCIENT HISTORY

....

1. 1895; 2. 22; 3. Batley; 4. Wales v New Zealand; 5. 1908/9;
6. Harold Buck; 7. The Nazis; 8. 1948; 9. 1954; 10. Puig Aubert;
11. Play-the-ball limit lowered to four tackles; 12. 1980

....

GREAT PLAYERS

....

1. St Helens; 2. Brian Bevan; 3. Mal Meninga; 4. 6,220;
5. Martin Offiah; 6. Shaun Edwards; 7. Dave Brown; 8. Billy Boston;
9. Puig Aubert; 10. Brad Fittler; 11. Jonathan Davies;
12. Roger Millward

....

ANSWERS
ATHLETICS

. . . .

RECORD BREAKERS: MEN

. . . .

1. 1997; 2. 3.43.13; 3. Usain Bolt; 4. Dayron Robles; 5. Jamaica;
6. Nesta Carter, Michael Frater, Usain Bolt and Asafa Powell;
7. Javelin; 8. Randy Barnes; 9. 1999; 10. 25,000m;
11. Haile Gebrselassie; 12. Javier Sotomayor

RECORD BREAKERS: WOMEN

. . . .

1. Svetlana Masterkova; 2. Half marathon and 20km; 3. Four;
4. 2:15:25; 5. Austra Skujyte; 6. Bulgarian; 7. 1988;
8. Olimpiada Ivanova; 9. 800m; 10. Wang Junxia; 11. USA; 12. 15.50m

NICKNAMES: WHO WAS KNOWN AS...?

. . . .

1. Fanny Blankers-Koen; 2. Paavo Nurmi; 3. Oscar Pistorius;
4. Merlene Ottey; 5. Steve Prefontaine; 6. Maurice Greene;
7. Alberto Juantorena; 8. Eric Liddell; 9. Florence Griffith Joyner;
10. Eamonn Coughlan; 11. Cornelius Warmerdam; 12. Carl Ludwig Long

STADIUMS AND TRACKS

. . . .

1. Crystal Palace; 2. Hyderabad; 3. Guadalajara, Mexico; 4. 2002;
5. Osaka; 6. Commonwealth Stadium; 7. Helsinki;
8. Hoosier Dome (Indiana); 9. Centennial Olympic Stadium;
10. Roger Bannister's sub-4 minute mile, 1954; 11. Gateshead;
12. The Netherlands

ANSWERS
ATHLETICS

89

ANCIENT HISTORY

1. 776 BC; 2. Royal Military College, Sandhurst;
3. The first modern Olympiad; 4. 1912; 5. British Empire Games;
6. Women were allowed to compete in track and field events; 7. Six;
8. 1954; 9. Boston Marathon; 10. 24; 11. 1960; 12. One, Running was
the only sport in the first 13 Olympics

TECHNICAL TERMS

1. The Fosbury Flop; 2. An arc across the track showing where runners
can break from lanes; 3. Seven; 4. 26.2miles (42.195km); 5. The line
marking the centre of the takeover zone; 6. On the takeoff board in
long or triple jumps: it shows where the jumper's foot has landed;
7. Long jump; 8. Did Not Finish; 9. Running variously at fast, moderate
and slow speeds; 10. The first runner in a relay team; 11. The leading
foot used by track or field athletes; 12. Passing the relay baton

QUOTES: WHO SAID...?

1. Zola Budd; 2. Roger Bannister; 3. Eamonn Martin;
4. Fatima Whitbread; 5. Carl Lewis; 6. Daley Thompson;
7. Abebe Bikila; 8. Dick Fosbury; 9. Marion Jones; 10. Al Oerter;
11. Jesse Owens; 12. Alberto Juantorena

NAME THE YEAR

1. 1984; 2. 1921; 3. 1956; 4. 2008; 5. 1988; 6. 1912; 7. 1986; 8. 1968;
9. 2004; 10. 1993; 11. 1960; 12. 1978

ANSWERS
ATHLETICS

....

OLYMPIC GAMES (1)

....

1. Wenlock Olympian Society; 2. Nine; 3. Five;
4. "Faster, Higher, Stronger"; 5. Olympia (Greece); 6. 204;
7. Jacques Rogge; 8. Berlin 1936; 9. Greece; 10. $100 million;
11. Jim Thorpe; 12. Because of the Suez Crisis

OLYMPIC GAMES (2)

....

1. Tommie Smith and John Carlos; 2. The Friendship Games;
3. First athlete to test positive for drug; 4. Brandy and strychnine;
5. 1972; 6. Gold-plated silver; 7. Paavo Nurmi and Carl Lewis (9);
8. Africa and South America; 9. Paris; 10. USA (4); 11. Spiridon Louis;
12. Avery Brundage

OLYMPIC GAMES (3)

....

1. 30th; 2. Greece; 3. She ran with men in the marathon; 4. Berlin;
5. Coca-Cola; 6. 1952; 7. Emil Zatopek; 8. 23; 9. Nadia Comaneci;
10. As protest at the Soviet invasion of Afghanistan;
11. Equatorial Guinean; 12. Steve Redgrave

OLYMPIC GAMES (4)

....

1. He won the 1500m and 5,000m on the same day;
2. Hicham el Guerrouj; 3. Tokyo; 4. Wilma Rudolph;
5. 5,000m and 10,000m; 6. Montreal 1976; 7. China; 8. Four;
9. Vitaly Scherbo (5); 10. 1976; 11. 400m; 12. Puerto Rico

ANSWERS
ATHLETICS

....

THE MARATHON

....

1. Vanderlei de Lima; 2. Dorando Pietri; 3. Paula Radcliffe;
4. Pheidippides; 5. Samuel Kamau Wanjiru; 6. Norway; 7. Ethiopian;
8. Most marathons run in a year (105); 9. Wales;
10. Charles Spedding; 11. Joan Benoit; 12. 1924

THE MILE AND 1500 METRES

....

1. Rome; 2. Yunxia Qu; 3. 1908; 4. 109m; 5. 1896; 6. Edwin Flack;
7. Steve Scott (136); 8. John Landy; 9. Svetlana Masterkova;
10. Steve Cram; 11. Rashid Ramzi; 12. Kenyan

SPRINTERS

....

1. Shell-Ann Fraser; 2. Canadian; 3. Wyomia Tyus; 4. 10.49 seconds; 5.
60m; 6. 37.10 seconds; 7. It is the length of the sprint track
at Olympia; 8. Seville; 9. Oscar Pistorius; 10. Marita Koch;
11. Only athlete to win both 400m and 800m at the same Games;
12. Christine Ohuruogo

DISTANCE RUNNING

....

1. 10,000m; 2. Haile Gebrselassie; 3. Ethiopian; 4. Kenenisa Bekele;
5. 17; 6. 12.5; 7. 10k; 8. 12; 9. Billy Mills; 10. Emil Zatopek;
11. Wang Junxia; 12. Mary Decker

ANSWERS
ATHLETICS

JUMPING

1. Cuban; 2. Stefka Kostadinova; 3. Four extra spikes in the heel;
4. Steve Smith; 5. 29.1ft (8.90m); 6. A weight in each hand;
7. Vilma Bardauskiene (1978); 8. Mike Powell; 9. It consisted of two
hops, then a jump; 10. Portuguese; 11. By distance (not height);
12. Sergey Bubka

JAVELIN, SHOT, DISCUS, HAMMER

1. 2.7m; 2. To reduce flight distance and make it stick in the ground;
3. Steve Backley; 4. 1984; 5. The "spin" style; 6. Parry O'Brien;
7. 74ft 3ins (22.63m); 8. No – only ancient; 9. Gabriele Reinsch;
10. Mac Wilkins; 11. A sledgehammer; 12. Yuriy Sedykh

ALL-ROUNDERS

1. C B Fry; 2. Babe Didrikson; 3. Menzies Campbell; 4. Jim Thorpe;
5. Lottie Dod; 6. Sebastian Coe; 7. Eric Liddell;
8. Jackie Joyner-Kersee; 9. Emil Zatopek; 10. Roger Bannister;
11. Chris Brasher; 12. Bob Hayes

GREAT ATHLETES

1. Finnish; 2. Kipchoge Keino; 3. Maria Mutola; 4. Don Quarrie;
5. Kenya and Denmark; 6. 18; 7. 40; 8. 1935; 9. Michael Johnson;
10. Iolanda Balas; 11. Jonathan Edwards; 12. Cathy Freeman

ANSWERS
CRICKET

....

RECORD BREAKERS

....

1. W G Grace, E; 2. Steve Waugh, A (168); 3. Hanif Mohammed (337 P v WI, 1958); 4. Sydney Barnes (49 E v SA, 1913/14); 5. 10 for 74 (Anil Kumble I v P, 1999); 6. Australia (4) 7. Chris Gayle (117 WI v SA, 2007); 8. 5th Test, South Africa v England, 1939 (10 days); 9. Ravi Shastri (Bombay v Baroda, 1985); 10. Mark Boucher, SA (475); 11. 624 by Kumar Sangakkara and Mahela Jayawardene (SL v SA, 2006); 12. Don Bradman, A (99.94)

....

NICKNAMES: WHO ARE...?

....

1. Michael Holding; 2. Harbhajan Singh; 3. Phil Tufnell; 4. Steve Waugh; 5. Gilbert Jessop; 6. Lance Klusener; 7. W.G.Grace; 8. Joel Garner; 9. Ted Dexter; 10. Sunil Gavaskar; 11. Fred Trueman; or Geoff Boycott; 12. Keith Miller

....

ALL-ROUNDERS

....

1. Denis Compton; 2. Sammy Woods; 3. Scunthorpe United; 4. C B Fry; 5. Mike Brearley; 6. J W H T Douglas; 7. Arthur Milton; 8. Samuel Beckett; 9. Imran Khan; 10. C Aubrey Smith; 11. Keith Miller; 12. Sir Learie Constantine

....

INITIALS: WHAT ARE THE FULL NAMES OF...?

....

1. Everton Weekes; 2. Bob Willis; 3. David Gower; 4. Gary Sobers; 5. Basil d'Oliveira; 6. Dennis Lillee; 7. Colin Cowdrey; 8. Glenn McGrath; 9. Ian Botham; 10. Kevin Pietersen; 11. Donald Bradman; 12. Bill O'Reilly

....

ANSWERS
CRICKET

....

ANCIENT HISTORY

....

1. Early batters defended tree stumps; 2. "Silver Billy"; 3. 1862;
4. Gloucestershire; 5. They were all Aboriginals; 6. After wicket gates
used as targets by early cricketers; 7. North America;
8. Charles Bannerman; 9. The googly (or "Bosie") 10. F S Jackson;
11. England; 12. Victor Trumper

....

LIMITED OVERS

....

1. The Gillette Cup; 2. Frank Duckworth and Tony Lewis;
3. India, Pakistan, Bangladesh and Sri Lanka; 4. Australia;
5. Afghanistan; 6. 443 for 9 by Sri Lanka v Netherlands, 2006;
7. Chaminda Vaas, 8 –19, SL v Zimbabwe, 2001; 8. Hat trick, for
Australia v Bangladesh; 9. Brendan McCullum, NZ; 10. Australia, 23,
2003; 11. England; 12. 229 by Belinda Clarke, A v Denmark, 1997

....

CRICKET QUOTES: WHO SAID...?

....

1. George Hirst, Oval, 1902; 2. Graham Dilley, Headingley, 1981;
3. Ernest Jones to W G Grace, Sheffield, 1896; 4. C L R James;
5. Brian Johnston; 6. Fred Trueman, Australia, 1958;
7. Robert Mugabe; 8. Vivian Richards; 9. Donald Bradman;
10. Derek Randall to Dennis Lillee, Melbourne, 1976; 11. Tony Greig
(of West Indies), 1976; 12. Denis Compton, frequently

....

IN THE FAMILY

....

1. Dean Headley; 2. Brothers; 3. Peter and Graeme; 4. Mark ("the
Forgotten") Waugh; 5. Richard Hadlee; 6. Edward Mills (EM) Grace;
7. The Hollioakes, Butchers and Bicknells; 8. Brother-in-law;
9. Liam Botham; 10. Ian and Greg Chappell, and Victor Richardson;
11. Javed Burki and Majid Khan; 12. Jim Troughton

....

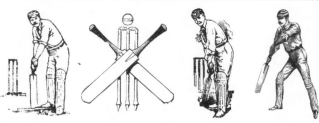

ANSWERS
CRICKET

. . . .

TECHNICAL TERMS

. . . .

1. From leg to off; 2. A full toss directed at the batsman's head;
3. A king pair; 4. From leg to off; 5. The part of the handle which fits
into the blade; 6. A delivery which stays very low; 7. Off side;
8. A ball bowled by a left-armer which moves from off to leg;
9. At right angles to the bowling crease; 10. A guard of middle-and-leg;
11. An off-break bowled with a leg-break action;
12. Carrying a cricketer's equipment

WHERE DO THEY PLAY?

. . . .

1. Port-of-Spain, Trinidad; 2. Nottinghamshire; 3. It was founded by
Thomas Lord; 4. The WACA (Western Australian Cricket Association);
5. Johannesburg, SA; 6. Saravanamuttu Oval, Colombo;
7. Riverside, Chester-le-Street; 8. Antigua; 9. The MCG in Melbourne, A;
10. Bombay, I ;11. Lancaster Park, Christchurch;
12. National Stadium, Karachi

GREAT BATTING

. . . .

1. Gilbert Jessop; 2. 1994; 3. Don Bradman; 4. 174; 5. V V S. Laxman;
6. Stan McCabe; 7. 2; 8. Jack Hobbs (197); 9. His second 100 was the
fastest Test century ever made (39 balls); 10. Everton Weekes (5);
11. Denis Compton (173, E v P, 1954); 12. Glamorgan

GREAT BOWLING

. . . .

1. 90; 2. Frederick Spofforth; 3. 9-121 by Arthur Mailey (AvE, 1921);
4. Gary Sobers; 5. Steve Harmison; 6. Anil Kumble, 10-74 (IvP, 1999);
7. Devon Malcolm (EvSA, 1994); 8. 1993; 9. Michael Holding;
10. Wilfred Rhodes (4,187); 11. Muttiah Muralitharan (currently 770);
12. 16

ANSWERS

CRICKET

....

LONG TERM, SHORT TERM

....

1. Wilfred Rhodes, 1898-1930; 2. Hassan Raza, 14 years, 227 days (pvZ, 1996); 3. Allan Border, 153; 4. 1,015 minutes by Rajiv Nayyar (271) for Himachal Pradesh v Jammu & Kashmir, 2000; 5. It was the shortest (a single match in 1925 lasting 165 minutes, where he neither batted or bowled); 6. 19 by Matabeleland v Mashonaland, 2001; 7. Timed out (Notts v Durham University); 8. 53 balls (Hants v Warks, 1922); 9. 0.96 per over, NzvE, 1955 (26 runs in 27 overs); 10. Bangladesh (23); 11. Wasim Akram (P), 18,186; 12. Trevor Bailey

....

ASHES SPECIAL

....

1. Uncertain: probably a bail, stump or ball; 2. A Waterford Crystal replica of the urn; 3. Douglas Jardine in 1932/33; 4. Eric Hollies; 5. Kim Hughes; 6. 3 runs; 7. Twice, by Australia (1920/21 and 2006/07); 8. 316; 9. Australia (131); 10. Don Bradman (A), 19; 11. Jim Laker (E), 46 in 1956; 12. Charles Bannerman (A), 1877

....

WHICH SURNAMES?

....

1. Hughes; 2. Jones; 3. Smith; 4. Butcher; 5. Richardson; 6. Richards; 7. Chappell; 8. Taylor; 9. Watson; 10. Murray; 11. Jackson; 12. Harris

....

IN THE FIELD

....

1. 1930; 2. Rahul Dravid (I), 184; 3. Kieran More, 5, IvWI, 1988; 4. Brett Lee, 3, AvSL, 2007; 5. Clive Lloyd; 6. Colin Cowdrey; 7. Bob Taylor, 1,649; 8. Wally Hammond, 10, Gloucs v Surrey, 1928; 9. Adam Gilchrist; 10. Marsh (Rodney); 11. Pakistan, 7 v A, 1972; 12. Mahela Jayawardene (SL), 159

....

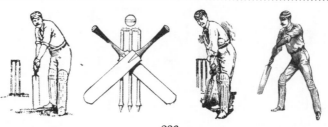

ANSWERS
CRICKET

. . . .

WORLD CUP

. . . .

1. West Indies; 2. South Africa; 3. Alvin Kallicharran; 4. 257 runs by India v Bermuda, 2007; 5. Australia (69); 6. Gary Kirsten, 188*, SA v UAE, 1996; 7. Glenn McGrath (A), 18.19; 8. 1983; 9. 318 by Rahul Dravid and Sourav Ganguly, I v SL, 1999; 10. England (3 times); 11. Stephen Fleming (NZ), 27; 12. Lance Klusener (SA), 124.00

. . . .

NUMBERS: WHAT'S THE SIGNIFICANCE OF...?

. . . .

1. Brian Lara's record first-class score; 2. "Nelson" – England's unlucky number; 3. Jim Laker's record wicket haul; 4. Date of the first Test Match; 5. Gary Sobers' Test record innings, which stood for 36 years; 6. Bob Willis' match-winning haul at Headingley in 1981; 7. Australia's unlucky number; 8. The year of Pakistan's first Test match; 9. Jack Hobbs' record first-class aggregate; 10. The amount by which Don Bradman missed a Test average of exactly 100; 11. Number taken by Viv Richards to score the fastest Test 100; 12. Gary Sobers' sequence of shots against Malcolm Nash in 1968

. . . .

WOMEN'S CRICKET

. . . .

1. 1934; 2. England; 3. 569-6 (AvE, 1998); 4. 1973; 5. 8; 6. Lord's; 7. Kiran Baluch (242), PvWI, 2004; 8. Patricia McKelvey (NZ), 14; 9. Mary Duggan (E), 77; 10. 22, Netherlands v WI, 2008; 11. 13-226 by Shaiza Khan (P v WI, 2004); 12. England (19)

. . . .

CUPS AND COMPETITIONS

. . . .

1. Surrey; 2. The Gillette Cup; 3. United Arab Emirates; 4. The Chappell – Hadlee Trophy; 5. The Pura Cup; 6. 1900; 7. Six; 8. Rajasthan Royals; 9. South Africa; 10. Pakistan; 11. Yorkshire (30); 12. 2000

. . . .

ANSWERS
GOLF

RECORD BREAKERS (1)

1. Ben Hogan and Tiger Woods; 2. Jack Nicklaus (18);
3. Nick Faldo (7); 4. One; 5. Lee Trevino and Tiger Woods;
6. Sam Snead (52 years old); 7. Al Geiburger (1977);
8. 19 (Ray Ainsley); 9.Tiger Woods; 10. Harry Vardon;
11. Young Tom Morris; 12. Vijay Singh

NICKNAMES – WHO WAS KNOWN AS...? (1)

1. Ernie Els; 2. Gary Player; 3. Sergio Garcia; 4. Jack Nicklaus;
5. Ben Hogan; 6. Arnold Palmer; 7. Walter Hagen; 8. Lee Trevino;
9. Gene Sarazen; 10. John Daly; 11. Jesper Parnevik; 12. Henry Picard

TECHNICAL TERMS

1. When hitting shots from the fairway; 2. A narrow-bladed club,
like a modern 4-iron; 3. Cavity back; 4. Covering golf balls;
5. The socket in the head for the shaft; 6. Skins; 7. When it is so close
to the hole as to be unmissable; 8. A free shot given to someone who
has played a bad one; 9. The most common overlapping grip (invented
by Harry Vardon); 10. A scuffed shot which goes little distance;
11. The green; 12. It gets stuck in wet sand or mud

ANCIENT HISTORY

1. Rabbit holes; 2. It is the oldest golf course in the world;
3. Charles I; 4. Scotland; 5. Gutt-percha; 6. 1898; 7. Old Tom Morris;
8. Bogey; 9. 1896; 10. Sunningdale; 11. John McDermott;
12. It exploded in hot weather

ANSWERS
GOLF

COURSES OF THE WORLD

1. St. Andrews; 2. The holes are dug in sand and oil, with no grass;
3. Thailand; 4. Son Gual; 5. Augusta; 6. Oakmont;
7. Valderrama; 8. William IV; 9. Muirfield; 10. Pine Valley;
11. Royal Melbourne; 12. Turnberry

QUOTES: WHO SAID...?

1. A A Milne; 2. P G Wodehouse; 3. Dean Martin; 4. Mark Twain;
5. Tiger Woods; 6. Gary Player; 7. Arnold Palmer; 8. Tom Watson;
9. Jack Nicklaus; 10. Lee Trevino; 11. Bob Hope; 12. Ben Hogan

NAME THE YEAR (1)

1. 1960; 2. 1943; 3. 1754; 4. 1916; 5. 1929; 6. 2007; 7. 1969; 8. 1997;
9. 2008; 10. 1934; 11. 1961; 12. 1951

THE OPEN

1. July; 2. They play a 4-hole playoff; 3. The Champions Belt;
4. Bobby Jones (1930); 5. Fred Daly (1947); 6. Jack Nicklaus (61);
7. 1995; 8. Prestwick; 9. Harry Vardon (6);
10. Young Tom Morris (17 years 181 days); 11. Old Tom Morris
(46 years 99 days); 12. Royal St George's

ANSWERS
GOLF

133

THE US OPEN

1. A 5th round is played; 2. Three; 3. Newport, Rhode Island;
4. Horace Rawling; 5. Tony Jacklin (1970); 6. The top 15 finishers from
the previous year; 7. Angel Cabrera; 8. He was the oldest champion;
9. Tiger Woods, 12 under (2000); 10. Congressional Country Club,
Bethesda; 11. Willie Anderson (3); 12. Willie Anderson, Bobby Jones,
Ben Hogan, Jack Nicklaus (4)

THE MASTERS

1. It is by invitation only; 2. Jack Nicklaus (6); 3. April; 4. Five;
5. 1934; 6. Gary Player (52); 7. He was the first African-American
to qualify; 8. None; 9. Trevor Immelman; 10. Nick Faldo (1996);
11. Nick Price and Greg Norman; 12. Tiger Woods (21 years 104 days)

THE PGA CHAMPIONSHIP

1. 1916; 2. Jim Barnes; 3. 1958; 4. Padraig Harrington;
5. Steve Elkington (1995); 6. Lionel Hebert; 7. Dow Finsterwald;
8. Gene Sarazen (20 years 174 days); 9. Atlanta Athletic Club, Georgia;
10. David Toms (265); 11. Walter Hagen and Jack Nicklaus (5);
12. The Wanamaker Trophy

136

WOMEN'S GOLF

1. 1976; 2. Ji-Yai Shin; 3. Mary, Queen of Scots; 4. 1894;
5. Lady Margaret Scott; 6. Babe Didrikson Zaharias (1946);
7. Annika Sorenstam (90); 8. Kraft Nabisco Championship;
9. Karrie Webb; 10. USA and Europe; 11. Nancy Lopez; 12. Michelle Wie

ANSWERS
GOLF

....

THE RYDER CUP

....

1. 1927; 2. 2001; 3. Bernhard Langer; 4. Three days; 5. Seed merchant;
6. 1969; 7. 1999; 8. 2002; 9. Seven; 10. Nick Faldo (11); 11. Scott
Verplank and Paul Casey; 12. Sergio Garcia (19 years 258 days)

....

CUPS AND TROPHIES

....

1. USA and a team from countries ineligible for the Ryder Cup;
2. Walker Cup; 3. Curtis Cup; 4. Japan Tour and Asia Tour players;
5. Under 30; 6. Royal Trophy; 7. Seve Trophy; 8. US and European
university golfers; 9. 16; 10. Lexus Cup; 11. 1959;
12. The Race to Dubai

....

GREAT GOLFERS

....

1. Walter Hagen; 2. Ben Hogan; 3. Colin Montgomerie;
4. Severiano Ballesteros; 5. Laura Davies; 6. Babe Didrikson
Zaharias; 7. Sam Snead (52 years 10 months); 8. J.H.Taylor;
9. "Arnie's Army"; 10. Tiger Woods; 11. Annika Sorenstam;
12. Because of his blond hair

....

RECORD BREAKERS (2)

....

1. 15 shots, by Tiger Woods (2000); 2. Vijay Singh, $10,905,166 (2004);
3. Annika Sorenstam, 59 (2001); 4. Jack Nicklaus (15);
5. Scottish (55); 6. Gary Player and Fred Couples (23);
7. Anthony Kim (11); 8. Greg Norman (267); 9. Only played over 36
holes; 10. Johnny Miller, Jack Nicklaus, Tom Weiskopf and Vijay
Singh (63); 11. Oakmont; 12. Julius Boros (48 years 142 days)

....

ANSWERS
GOLF

· ·

THE EUROPEAN TOUR

· ·

1. 1901; 2. The Tunisian Open (1982); 3. 1989; 4. Bangkok;
5. Robert Karlsson; 6. Colin Montgomerie (8); 7. Ian Poulter;
8. Lee Westwood; 9. Colin Montgomerie (4); 10. Severiano Ballesteros;
11. 1979; 12. Gwladys Nocera

THE PGA TOUR

· ·

1. Florida; 2. 1975; 3. Scotland; 4. The Mercedes-Benz Championship;
5. The Memorial Tournament; 6. Vijay Singh; 7. Tiger Woods (4);
8. China; 9. Jim Barnes (3); 10. 1916; 11. Jack Nicklaus and Tiger
Woods (8); 12. Andres Romero

NAME THE YEAR (2)

· ·

1. 1979; 2. 1964; 3. 1991; 4. 1989 and 1990; 5. 1896 (James Foulis);
6. 2006; 7. 1890 (John Ball Jr); 8. 1976; 9. 1991; 10. 2009; 11. 1904;
12. 1986

NICKNAMES – WHO WAS KNOWN AS...? (2)

· ·

1. Mildred Didrikson Zaharias; 2. Michelle Wie; 3. David Duval;
4. Eduardo Romero; 5. Tony Lema; 6. Craig Stadler; 7. Paul Azinger;
8. Sam Snead; 9. Jack Nicklaus; 10. Phil Mickelson; 11. Ben Hogan;
12. Tom Watson

ANSWERS
FOOTBALL: AWAY

....

WORLD CUP (1)

....

1. Scotland; 2. Giovanni Ferrari and Giuseppe Meazza;
3. Teofilo Cubilas; 4. Chicago; 5. Portugal (1966) and Croatia (1998);
6. Morocco; 7. Mexico; 8. Ed de Goey; 9. Alberto Supicci; 10. Seven;
11. Marcelo Salas; 12. Sweden

....

NICKNAMES – WHO WERE...? (1)

....

1. Ferenc Puskas; 2. Franz Beckenbauer; 3. Eric Cantona;
4. Jackie Charlton; 5. Edgar Davids; 6. Garrincha; 7. Ruud Gullit;
8. Jimmy Johnstone; 9. Stuart Pearce; 10. Gianni Rivera; 11. Tostao;
12. Ian Wright

....

AROUND THE WORLD (1)

....

1. Wynton Rufer; 2. Romania; 3. Bayern Munich; 4. Bergamo;
5. Inter Milan; 6. Miguel Munoz; 7. Penarol; 8. IFK Gothenburg;
9. Independiente; 10. Never; 11. Sardinia; 12. Burkina Faso

....

WHERE DO THEY PLAY?

....

1. Florence; 2. The Maracana; 3. Royal Antwerp; 4. FC Copenhagen;
5. Hamburg; 6. Camp Nou, Barcelona (98,000); 7. Torino;
8. May Day Stadium, Pyongyang, N. Korea (150,000); 9. Real Madrid;
10. Eindhoven; 11. Genoa; 12. Mexico

....

ANSWERS
FOOTBALL: AWAY

GOALKEEPERS & GOALSCORERS

1. Gianpiero Combi and Dino Zoff; 2. Toto Schillaci; 3. Sergio Goycochea; 4. Eusebio; 5. France; 6. Dutch; 7. Alfredo di Stefano; 8. Stern John (68); 9. Moscow Dynamo; 10. Oliver Kahn; 11. Landon Donovan (37); 12. Paolo Rossi

WORLD CUP (2)

1. 1962; 2. Gary Lineker; 3. Australia; 4. Joe Jordan; 5. Romania; 6. Ascot; 7. Switzerland; 8. Italy; 9. Mario Zagallo (Brazil) and Franz Beckenbauer (Germany); 10. Ronaldo (Brazil), 15; 11. Antonio Carbajal (Mexico) and Lothar Matthäus (Germany), five; 12. Most goals in a single tournament (13)

CLUB NICKNAMES: WHO ARE KNOWN AS...?

1. Wimbledon; 2. Aberdeen; 3. West Bromwich Albion; 4. Watford; 5. Partick Thistle; 6. Stirling Albion; 7. Albion Rovers; 8. Ivory Coast; 9. Barcelona; 10. Fiorentina; 11. Bayern Munich; 12. Benfica

FOOTBALL IN EUROPE

1. Lille; 2. Real Madrid; 3. Belgium; 4. Austria; 5. Malta; 6. Juventus; 7. Dan Eggen; 8. Luxembourg; 9. Cagliari; 10. Denmark; 11. Alfredo di Stefano; 12. Edgar Davids

ANSWERS
FOOTBALL: AWAY

AROUND THE WORLD (2)

1. 1994; 2. Athletico Bilbao; 3. Argentinian; 4. CSKA Sofia; 5. 1966;
6. Union Berlin; 7. Bolivia; 8. Gold with green trim;
9. Roberto Carlos; 10. Hamburg; 11. Cesare; 12. Spartak Moscow

LATIN AMERICA

1. São Paulo; 2. 1916; 3. Uruguay; 4. Brazil; 5. Argentina;
6. Copa Libertadores; 7. Tele Santana; 8. Venezuela;
9. Daniel Passarella; 10. White with a red stripe; 11. Roberto Rivelino;
12. 1977

CHAMPIONS' LEAGUE

1. 1955; 2. 1992; 3. 7 million euros; 4. Real Madrid;
5. Red Star Belgrade; 6. AC Milan 3, Liverpool 0; 7. Marseille;
8. Glentoran; 9. Bayern Munich; 10. Galatasaray; 11. Panathinaikos;
12. Michel Platini

WOMEN'S FOOTBALL

1. The Munitionettes' Cup (1917); 2. 1921; 3. 1982; 4. China;
5. USA; 6. Netherlands; 7. Copa la Reina (Queen's Cup);
8. *Bend It Like Beckham*; 9. Africa; 10. Arsenal; 11. Brazil;
12. Cristiane Rozeira de Souza Silva (Brazil) 5

ANSWERS

EUROPEAN CHAMPIONSHIP

1. 1960; 2. France; 3. Germany (3); 4. None; 5. Michel Platini (9);
6. Tomas Brolin; 7. Hungary; 8. They were technically still at war;
9. 44; 10. David Villa (4); 11. Romania; 12. Dennis Bergkamp and
Glenn Helder

WORLD CUP (3)

1. Zaire; 2. Czechoslovakia and Bulgaria; 3. New Zealand;
4. Bernard Voorhof; 5. Ferenc Puskas; 6. Walter Zenga;
7. Claudio Caniggia; 8. Pele; 9. First substitute in World Cup finals
(1970); 10. 18; 11. Seven; 12. Portugal

NICKNAMES – WHO WERE...? (2)

1. Tony Adamas; 2. Roberto Baggio; 3. Marcel Desailly;
4. Eusebio; 5. Mark Hughes; 6. Filippo Inzaghi; 7. Attilio Lombardo;
8. Stanley Matthews; 9. Ronaldo; 10. Teddy Sheringham;
11. Hristo Stoichkov; 12. Lev Yashin

AROUND THE WORLD (3)

1. AEK Athens; 2. Nigeria; 3. Brazil; 4. Oleg Blokhin; 5. Toulon;
6. 1990; 7. Tunisia; 8. Borussia Monchengladbach; 9. Hristo Stoichkov;
10. He won the 3 main European cup competitions – with 3 different
teams; 11. One (2002); 12. Albert Camus

ANSWERS
OTHER TEAM SPORTS

. . . .

BASEBALL (1)

. . . .

1. He wrote the first published rules; 2. Cincinnati Red Stockings;
3. 60ft 6ins (18.4m); 4. They are the oldest team in US organized
sports; 5. .367; 6. "Georgia Peach"; 7. 1903; 8. Eight;
9. Walter Johnson; 10. New York Yankees (26);
11. Replacement of discoloured balls; 12. George Herman Ruth

BASEBALL (2)

. . . .

1. Shortest-ever Major League player; 2. His own; 3. 1939; 4. 56;
5. Jackie Robinson; 6. 1947; 7. Carl Yastrzemski; 8. Dick Allen;
9. Luke Appling; 10. 1998; 11. 1994; 12. Cal Ripken Jr

BASEBALL (3)

. . . .

1. Joe DiMaggio; 2. Phil Niekro; 3. Great Britain; 4. Barry Bonds (762);
5. Nolan Ryan (383); 6. Rickey Henderson (1,406); 7. James Bell;
8. An easy catch for a fielder; 9. Lou Gehrig; 10. Stan Musial;
11. Hank Aaron; 12. Yogi Berra

HOCKEY (1)

. . . .

1. *Hocquet* (a shepherd's crook); 2. Ireland and Wales; 3. 1908;
4. India; 5. Shinty; 6. 12ft (3.66m); 7. Netherlands; 8. Lahore;
9. Sean Kerly (64); 10. First Australian Aboriginal to win Olympic gold;
11. Ric Charlesworth; 12. 1976

ANSWERS

OTHER TEAM SPORTS

....

HOCKEY (2)

....

1. Germany; 2. Pakistan (4); 3. Runners-up (1986); 4. 6-2;
5. Australia and Germany; 6. Korea; 7. Rechelle Hawkes;
8. Richard Leman (158); 9. 100yd (91.4m); 10. Dhyan Chand; 11. Three;
12. A player passes to another, who immediately passes back (to
bypass an opponent)

....

ICE HOCKEY (1)

....

1. Canada; 2. 1920; 3. Great Britain; 4. "puc" (to poke or punch);
5. Montreal; 6. 1972; 7. Defence; 8. Erwin Chamberlain; 9. 1930;
10. New York Rangers; 11. 6ft (1.82m); 12. Sweden

....

ICE HOCKEY (2)

....

1. 20 mins; 2. Sidney Crosby; 3. Montreal Canadiens; 4. 1999;
5. Jabbing an opponent with the stick shaft; 6. A goal, an assist and
a fight; 7. Czech; 8. 894; 9. Henri Richard; 10. A decoy or feint;
11. Tony Hand (119); 12. The Stanley Cup

....

AMERICAN FOOTBALL (1)

....

1. 100yds (91.4m); 2. 1967; 3. Harvard v Yale; 4. Walter Camp; 5. 19;
6. Knute Rockne; 7. Jim Brown; 8. Red Grange; 9. Offensive and
defensive lines; 10. Vince Lombardi Trophy; 11. Joe Namath;
12. William Perry

....

ANSWERS
OTHER TEAM SPORTS

. . . .

AMERICAN FOOTBALL (2)

. . . .

1. A high pass throne to the end zone at the finish of a half; 2. 34;
3. First recorded professional player; 4. Elroy Hirsch; 5. Jim Thorpe;
6. 1920; 7. Baltimore Colts v NY Giants (1958); 8. Jerry Rice (208);
9. Walter Payton; 10. George Blanda (26); 11. Drew Bledsoe (70);
12. Pittsburgh Steelers (6)

. . . .

AMERICAN FOOTBALL (3)

. . . .

1. Gerald Ford; 2. Norm Van Brocklin; 3. The officials;
4. Arlington, Texas; 5. Curly Lambeau; 6. O J Simpson; 7. Jim Thorpe;
8. Denmark; 9. George Halas; 10. London Monarchs; 11. 1970;
12. Arizona Cardinals

. . . .

AUSTRALIAN RULES FOOTBALL

. . . .

1. Oval; 2. To keep cricketers fit in winter; 3. 1897; 4. Collingwood
(1927-30); 5. 15m; 6. March; 7. Adelaide; 8. Tony Lockett (1,360);
9. Michael Tuck (426); 10. Fred Fanning (18.1); 11. Keith Bromage
(15 years 287 days); 12. 37.17.239 (Geelong 1992)

. . . .

GAELIC FOOTBALL AND HURLING

. . . .

1. Ireland and Australia; 2. 1887; 3. He releases the ball
and then kicks it back into his hands; 4. Kevin Heffernan;
5. Croke Park, Dublin; 6. Kerry (35); 7. 15; 8. Camogie;
9. Kilkenny (31); 10. The ball; 11. Christy Ring; 12. Jack Lynch

. . . .

ANSWERS
OTHER TEAM SPORTS

··

BASKETBALL (1)

··

1. 1891; 2. A peach basket; 3. A soccer ball; 4. 1946; 5. Sudanese;
6. Japan; 7. 94ft (28m); 8. Shaquille O'Neal; 9. To commit a personal
foul; 10. Philadelphia Warriors; 11. 1936; 12. Gheorghe Muresan and
Manute Bol (7ft 7ins, 2.31m)

··

BASKETBALL (2)

··

1. French; 2. George Gervin; 3. 1984; 4. Wilt Chamberlain (100);
5. Dominique Wilkins (23); 6. 38,387; 7. Detroit Pistons v Denver
Nuggets (370 in 1983); 8. Michael Jordan (11); 9. 33 games (LA
Lakers 1971-2); 10. Bob Pettit; 11. Darryl Dawkins; 12. Larry Kenon
and Kendall Gill (11)

··

BASKETBALL (3)

··

1. Nathan Jawai; 2. Walt Bellamy (88); 3. Kevin Johnson (62);
4. Darrell Griffith; 5. 58 by Wilt Chamberlain (twice in 1960);
6. Michael Jordan (38 years 315 days); 7. Jerry West (1,679);
8. Boston Celtics (17); 9. Three; 10. Dennis Rodman;
11. Newcastle Eagles; 12. Dwight Howard (9)

··

LACROSSE

··

1. Iroquois; 2. Australia; 3. Ten; 4. Canada; 5. An indoor version of
the game; 6. Manchester; 7. Australia; 8. 1908; 9. England;
10. Only men; 11. 60 minutes; 12. Gary and Paul Gait (10)

··

. . . .

MIXED BAG (1)

. . . .

1. Thailand; 2. Loses 0 –13; 3. The target ball; 4. W G Grace;
5. David Bryant; 6. The bowl closest to the jack; 7. He lost; 8. 1900;
9. The part of the hoop below ground; 10. Chris Clarke;
11. White trousers and coloured shirts; 12. The *cesta*

MIXED BAG (2)

. . . .

1. 300yds (274m); 2. Seven-and-a-half minutes; 3. Chile;
4. As a less energetic alternative to basketball; 5. Italy; 6. 1996;
7. Seven; 8. Hungary; 9. Netball; 10. Sweden; 11. Le jeu provençal;
12. The jack

MIXED BAG (3)

. . . .

1. The time a kick stays in the air; 2. George "The Gipper" Gipp;
3. A player who runs the ball out of defence; 4. Four; 5. 10ft (3.05m);
6. Pete Rose (4,256); 7. "The Say Hey Kid"; 8. Minneapolis;
9. Tony Allcock; 10. The group of balls round the jack; 11. 1947;
12. Croatia

MIXED BAG (4)

. . . .

1. Five; 2. Above knee high; 3. 1936; 4. Between the goal-tender's
leg-pads; 5. One; 6. The ball travels at up to 186mph (300km/h);
7. Alexander the Great and Genghis Khan; 8. London debtors'
prisons; 9. Real tennis; 10. The stick for striking the ball;
11. Softball; 12. 1956

ANSWERS
OTHER INDIVIDUAL SPORTS

BOXING (1)

1. Cassius Clay (Muhammad Ali); 2. Over their hands and wrists;
3. Jack Dempsey; 4. Jim Corbett; 5. 1867; 6. One minute;
7. Archie Moore; 8. Duk Koo Kim; 9. Win titles in three different
weight classes; 10. Bob Fitzsimmons (1903); 11. Swedish law banned it;
12. Teofilo Stevenson

BOXING (2)

1. USA (109); 2. None; 3. Vitali and Wladimir Klitschko;
4. Edwin Valero; 5. 1921; 6. Evander Holyfield; 7. A clumsy or
unskilled fighter; 8. Sugar Ray Robinson; 9. Zaire;
10. Henry Armstrong; 11. Roberto Duran; 12. Riddick Bowe

BOXING (3)

1. Audley Harrison; 2. A rabbit punch; 3. Tony Galento;
4. Jack Johnson; 5. Gene Tunney; 6. John Douglas; 7. 1997;
8. 200.6lb (91kg); 9. Kazakhstani; 10. Joe Calzaghe; 11. Joe Louis;
12. 1965

GYMNASTICS

1. 2000; 2. Maria Petrova; 3. Lands perfectly without foot movement;
4. 14; 5. 1928; 6. Olga Korbut; 7. "Naked"; 8. China; 9. Nastia Liukin;
10. A back handspring in which the hands don't touch the floor;
11. 17; 12. 1.35m

ANSWERS
OTHER INDIVIDUAL SPORTS

. . . .

TABLE TENNIS

. . . .

1. 1988; 2. 9ft (2.74m); 3. Wang Hao; 4. London; 5. A simple racket grip which resembles shaking hands; 6. Viktor Barna; 7. Germany; 8. Zhang Yining; 9. Angelica Rozeanu; 10. The raised rubber dots on a bat's surface; 11. Cigar box lids; 12. 1971

SQUASH

. . . .

1. It is a super-slow ball used in championships; 2. Heather McKay; 3. Jansher Khan (8); 4. A ball played first off side or back walls; 5. Egyptian; 6. Nicol David; 7. Never (under consideration for 2016); 8. England; 9. Jahangir Khan; 10. Saudi Arabia; 11. David Palmer; 12. Geoff Hunt

SNOOKER

. . . .

1. 15; 2. Billiards; 3. 147; 4. Ronnie O'Sullivan (5mins 20 secs); 5. It rattles in the pocket before going down; 6. 1927; 7. Joe Davis; 8. James Wattana; 9. Stephen Hendry (732); 10. Ken Doherty (Ireland) and Cliff Thorburn (Canada); 11. John Parrott (1992); 12. John Higgins

DARTS

. . . .

1. 7ft 9¼in (2.37m); 2. Nine; 3. 1978; 4. Leighton Rees; 5. Keith Deller; 6. Ted Hankey; 7. Phil Taylor (14); 8. Dennis Priestley; 9. Dartitis; 10. One; 11. 1962; 12. Trina Gulliver

. . . .

BADMINTON

. . . .

1. Leather; 2. 5ft (1.55m); 3. 15; 4. It was launched at Badminton
House, Gloucs, UK; 5. 1977; 6. Rudy Hartono Kurniawan (8);
7. Danish; 8. 16; 9. Fu Haifeng (206mph (332km/h) in 2005); 10. 1992;
11. China (8); 12. Lin Dan

FENCING

. . . .

1. Foil *épée* and sabre; 2. Protective clothing to guard the sword arm
and side; 3. Edoardo Mangiarotti; 4. 1921; 5. The guard protecting a
fencer's fingers; 6. None: the whole body is a target; 7. Italy (21);
8. 1904; 9. Five; 10. Benjamin Kleibrink; 11. Ilona Elek; 12. Paris

CURLING

. . . .

1. The Stirling Stone; 2. 44lbs (20kg); 3. The house; 4. Because of the
roaring sound made by a stone on ice; 5. It is the oldest active sports
club in North America; 6. 1924; 7. Canada; 8. Rhona Martin;
9. 150ft (46m); 10. Concave; 11. Scotland; 12. Ailsa Craig

WRESTLING

. . . .

1. Henry VIII and Francis I; 2. No holding below the belt; 3. 2004;
4. Martin Klein v Alfred Asikainen (11 hours 40 minutes, 1912);
5. A freestyle move in which a wrestler entwines his legs around his
opponent's; 6. Five; 7. Carl Schuhmann; 8. Noel Loban (1984);
9. The outer circle of the wrestling mat; 10. None; 11. Mijain Lopez;
12. Mickey Rourke

ANSWERS
OTHER INDIVIDUAL SPORTS

. . . .

SHOOTING

. . . .

1. 1900; 2. Trap, double trap and skeet; 3. Zhang Shan (1992);
4. Pierre de Coubertin; 5. Karoly Takacs; 6. 50m; 7. 17 (2004);
8. 1904 and 1928; 9. Katerina Emmons; 10. India's first individual
gold medal; 11. Double trap and skeet; 12. Walton Eller

. . . .

WEIGHTLIFTING

. . . .

1. London; 2. Snatch and clean-and-jerk; 3. Ding Meiyuan;
4. Iranian; 5. Vassiliy Alekseyev; 6. 586.4lb (266kg) (Leonid Taranenko);
7. Naim Suleymanoglu; 8. John Davis; 9. Raising the barbell from the
floor until the lifter is upright; 10. The lifter with the lowest
body weight; 11. China (8); 12. He badly dislocated his elbow.

. . . .

DIVING

. . . .

1. 10m; 2. Synchronized diving; 3. 1904; 4. The plunge;
5. Chen Ruolin; 6. Tom Daley; 7. Greg Louganis; 8. Leon Taylor and
Peter Waterfield (2004); 9. USA (21); 10. None; 11. Matthew Mitcham;
12. The diver starts from a handstand

. . . .

JUDO

. . . .

1. "The gentle way"; 2. Ippon; 3. Jigoro Kano; 4. judogi; 5. 1964;
6. Karen Briggs; 7. Peter Sellers; 8. Albert of Monaco;
9. Shokichi Natsui; 10. Netherlands (1961); 11. Anton Geesink (1961);
12. The contestants stop fighting and freeze their positions

ANSWERS
OTHER INDIVIDUAL SPORTS

OTHER MARTIAL ARTS

1. "The Way to Harmonize with the Energy of the Universe";
2. The samurai; 3. Great Britain; 4. Kentsui; 5. Shotokan;
6. A karate master; 7. Kendo; 8. Kickboxing; 9. Alexei Tokarev;
10. China; 11. Jet Li; 12. Taekwondo

ICE SKATING

1. 1893; 2. Norway (36); 3. A one-legged spin with the other leg held
horizontally behind; 4. Katarina Witt; 5. Shani Davis (1:41.80);
6. Five; 7. 1984; 8. John Curry; 9. Alexander Zaitsev;
10. Shizuka Arakawa; 11. Two; 12. Tara Lipinski (15 years 257 days)

MIXED BAG (1)

1. The last shot in a contest; 2. Frank Hashman; 3. Alex Marshall;
4. Barry McGuigan; 5. James "Buster" Douglas;
6. The centre of the "house"; 7. 5ft 8ins (1.7m); 8. Pockets;
9. Double one; 10. 1976; 11. Ryoko Tani; 12. Kyu

MIXED BAG (2)

1. Portugal; 2. Taolu; 3. USA (2,193); 4. Stoke Mandeville, UK;
5. Rudolph Wanderone Jr.; 6. James Stout; 7. England;
8. Prone, kneeling and standing; 9. Steve Davis; 10. 10,000m;
11. Yang Yang (2002); 12. Blue